by Nataša Pantović
Ivana Milosavljević

Conscious Parenting Mindful Living Course for Parents

Alchemy of Love Mindfulness Training Course
http://www.artof4elements.com

Introduction to Self-Development Course Conscious Parenting

Our purpose is *to help you grow as a conscious human being.*

Conscious Parenting Mothering as Spiritual Quality

We hope to help you discover Your Self; inspire you to live more passionate and sensitive life; helping you listen to your Soul, finding your-own space in this matrix of life, making a genuine contribution to humanity.

Parenting is an Art Form

A very difficult one! We live surrounded by an increasingly complex matrix of impulses allowing strangers of all sorts (TV, media, Internet) interfere in our children's mental, emotional and spiritual development. Understanding this intricate network and how does the human brain interacts with it is increasingly becoming our door to happiness and health.

The self or the personality is a bundle of socially influenced traits that emerges and gets formed gradually. We are shaped by our parents and neighbors, by our religion, the media, by various marketing agendas of major corporations, by our state's politics, by the way we behave or misbehave towards our-own body, our mind, environment, animals and plants, and our planet Earth.

So, what would we need to do to understand the importance of a healthy body, to manage our emotions and nurture love for our friends and family, to become aware of how we can help ourselves and our children make a positive impact on our society or the environment, or discover the purpose of life and ways to be happy?

We hope to help you in your **Personal Development Journey** and encourage you to take full responsibility for your body and health, your mind, your emotions, your habits, your relationships, and your spiritual beliefs. We invite you to take the full responsibility for the growth of your children, and the happiness of your family.

Contents Various self-development Family Activities and Workshops

Introduction to Self-Development Course Conscious Parenting...2

Parenting is an art form 3

Conscious Parenting Self Development Course Methodology 11

Commitment Contract 14

Conscious Parenting Main Principles 16

Love Rhythm and Priorities 17

Priorities 24

Love 34

Module 1 Body 44

Observe Your Nutrition 45

Personality Questionnaire 1 Your attitude towards your body 51

Exercise 1 Defining your Areas for Improvement 56

Exercise 2 Rhythm and Food 60

Exercise 3 Create Your Dream Healthy Menu 70

Exercise 4 Breaking Stereotypes 72

Module 2 Your Home 74

Observe Your Attitude towards your Home 76

Questionnaire 1 Describing Your Environment..81

Exercise 1 Defining Areas of Improvement within Your Home 84

Exercise 3 Conscious Use of Colors 91

Exercise 4 Implement Simple Feng Shui Tips for Your Holistic Home 93

Module 3 Conscious & Unconscious Thinking 95

Happiness Test, Conscious Parenting Self Development Course..98

Questionnaire 1 Your Thinking Patterns 102

Exercise 1: My World, Our World...107

Exercise 2 Identify Your Mental Fixations 108

Exercise 3: Be Mindful..121

Exercise 4 Train Your Will Power...123

Exercise 5: Practice Concentration and Focus 126

Exercise 6: Draw Your Mandala 131

Task 1 Start with your Daily Meditation..136

Human Brain and its Magic 137

Practice Creativity 144

Module 4 Time / Life Wasters 146

Questionnaire 1 Your Time Wasters 147

Exercise 1: Master Your Daily Habits..151

Human Brain and Technology 153

Exercise 2: De-clutter and Simplify 155

Module 5 Feelings 157

Observe Your Feelings..158

Exercise 1: Exercise Awareness 164

Exercise 2: Your Soul's Diary 166

Exercise 3: Practice Virtues 167

Module 6 Core Beliefs 170

Understanding Core Beliefs..172

Questionnaire 1 My Core Beliefs 175

Exercise 1 What are your LIMITING BELIEFS 178

Exercise 2 Draw a Flower of Beliefs 181

Exercise 3 My Name 181

Exercise 4 Challenge Existing Beliefs 183

Module 7 Relationships 185

Questionnaire 1 Relationship Questionnaire 186

Exercise 2: Are You Truly Listening?...193

Exercise 3 Exercise Conscious Speech 195

Exercise 4: Secret Gift...198

Exercise 5: Circle of Love 198

Exercise 6: Learn about Each Other and Have Fun 199

Exercise 7: Your Relationship Plan 203

Exercise 8: Express Freedom ... 207
Module 8 Our Greater Surrounding ... 208
Questionnaire 1 Our Greater Surrounding ... 209
Exercise 1 Change the Word ... 213
Exercise 2 I have the power to change the world ... 213
Exercise 2: Service ... 216
Module 9 Your Dreams ... 218
Exercise 1 Identify Your True Dreams ... 220
Questionnaire 1 Your True Dreams ... 223
Questionnaire 2 Your Child's Dreams ... 228
Module 10 Your True Goals ... 229
Exercise 1 Your Personal Development Plan ... 230
Module 11 Spirituality ... 233
Exercise 1 What is Karma? ... 234
Exercise 1 So What is Karma For You? ... 234
Exercise 2: Your Spiritual Diary ... 235
Module 12 Spirituality & You ... 239
Exercise 1 Have Divine as the main focus all through your day ... 240
Exercise 2 Drumming, Meditation, Yoga Circle ... 241
Exercise 3 Enter Your Dream World ... 241
Exercise 4 Seek Spiritual Company ... 244
List of Recommended Books ... 245
Our Children ... 246
Will we learn from Finland? ... 248
Education of the future ... 250
Arts make students smart, Children and Creativity ... 251
Inspiring children with arts, music, sport ... 252
Schools that inspire children to learn – dream or reality? ... 255
List of Articles for Your further Inspiration ... 257

Title	Description of Transfrmation Tools
MODULE 1 Attitude towards Body	We will help you examine your body, your health, your exercise regime, the food that you eat, your habits and patterns.
MODULE 2, Attitude towards Home	We will help you examine your home, the environment that surrounds you, your habits and patterns.
MODULE 3, Thinking Patterns	Examine your Mind and your every-day thoughts. Look into your conscious and sub-conscious addictions, identify your strengths and weaknesses.
MODULE 4, Time / Life Wasters	Often we waste time unconsciously and we need to apply a conscious effort to record this time and activities, so that we become aware of the wasters of our life
Module 5, FREE MIND: Your Feelings	We will help you examine your world of feelings and emotions.
Module 6, Your Core Beliefs	Your enemy within are your core negative beliefs. Negative beliefs hide from the consciousness & they get exposed by the magic of mindfulness and awareness.
Module 7, Relationships	You will examine your relationships, your **ability to love** and tune into your-own and other people's wants and needs
Module 8, Your Greater Surrounding	We live in our Greater Surrounding. Our capability for love grows and expands into our surroundings – Earth, animals, plants, our neighbors, strangers.
Module 9, Your Dreams	Turn away from your dream and it will come back to you. **Follow your dream** and it will give you a **tremendous amount of pleasure and learning**.
Module 10, Your True Goals	Identify your **True Goals** and Actions to achieve them… **Listen to your Heart and follow your Mind**!
Module 11, Spirituality	What is Spirituality for you? Start your **Spiritual Diary** and get inspired within your Spiritual Journey
Module 12, Your Spiritual Journey	Meditate, start your **Dreams Diary**, Read Spiritual Books, Seek Spiritual Company.

ALL THROUGHOUT THE EXERCISES YOU AND YOUR CHILD WILL BE EXPLORING:

Concentration: Learn the art of concentration and practice with your children 'focus' that will help you grow and do your day-to-day duties the best you can.
Will-Power: Work with the magic of discipline to create the life you desire
Love: Improve your ability to connect with yourself and others
Creative Intelligence: Live authentically, and express your creativity
Listen to Your Soul: Learn how to listen to your Soul' Whispers
Oneness: Realise that we are all One
Spirituality: Raise your awareness and live more consciously

So, why Self Development?

Self-development is a way of Life. **Our Self Development never ends.** We are never too young or too old for personal growth.

We have an amazing potential to reach our highest potential, to have truly inspiring careers and loving relationships.

Unfortunately, often we walk through our lives asleep, we let our habits rule us, and find it difficult to change our beliefs. Recognizing the power of our Mind and the power of our Soul, learning the art of Concentration and Love, we are learning to Live with the Flow, not against it.

It is in our **nature to learn and grow**. For happiness we need to learn to Love, we need to learn to Concentrate and we should keep the flow and energy of inspiration within our lives. Taking a commitment to grow, work on Self, spiritually develop, we **take responsibility for our lives.**

Learning the art of **Self Development** we learn about **power of mind**, **consciousness**, **mindfulness**, **true love**, and we become aware of the possibility to live life in harmony with ourselves, our family, neighbors, our relatives, our parents, animals, plants, and the planet Earth. Through a process of **self-discovery**, we will learn mindfulness, we will get in touch with conscious behavior and change our attitudes so that we are not ruled by instincts, habits and someone else beliefs.

Our Soul is the true driver of the chariot called our body and mind, and it is a source of an amazing inner knowing.

Why Self Development for Parents?

Because **the world belongs to our children** and we are their soil, their water, their air.

Because the parenting IS the most difficult job in the world

Because it is possible to get it RIGHT, our children need our Love, but also our support within this amazing matrix of choices. They need us to guide them towards healthy foods, healthy habits, inspiring activities, life enriching friends, etc.

It is unfortunately easy for parents to lose themselves in RESPONSIBILITY, in day to day tasks, in screams of demanding children, within the piles of shit of their babies, within

RULES they are supposed to follow and within ROLES they are supposed to play. It is easy for parents to lose the connection with **Her Majesty Love**.

No matter how much we try we will not get it RIGHT the first time, we (human beings) need to GO through an experience to be able to learn. Helping a sister, who just had a child, is still a completely different experience form having your own child. The one who has never been a parent will have difficulties understanding all the struggles, traumas and complications, a parent needs to go through in his or her role of a Parent.

'**BECAUSE THE PARENTING IS THE MOST DIFFICULT JOB IN THE WORLD**

Our children need our **Love**, but also our support within this amazing matrix of choices. They need us to **guide them** towards **Healthy Foods**, **Healthy Habits**, **Inspiring Activities**, Life Enriching Friends, etc.'

www.artof4elements.com

However, it is possible to get it RIGHT the second, the third or perhaps the twenty-fourth time round. It is important not to give up, get discouraged, or forget that we can aim to reach our highest potential even surrounded with screams, buttered with no sleep, exhausted with the utter lack of privacy, utter lack of space for one-Self, constantly challenged with various demands (for more and more chocolate, for more and more TV, for more and more games, for more and more expensive gifts, for more and more and more). It is possible to get it RIGHT if we stick to the very basic principle of **Self Development** and **Spiritual Growth** let Her **Majesty Love** rule sharing the throne with her lover **Willpower**.

Conscious Parenting Self Development Course Methodology

Balancing Four Elements

The four elements within each one of us are: air, earth, fire, and water, four states of matter Life chooses to manifest on Earth: Jung describes them as four basic components of a personality: **intuition, sensation, thinking and feeling**.

In an attempt to deeper explore the infinite game of Life, together with you, we will explore:

- **Earth** that is fixed, rigid, static and quiet, and symbolizes your **world of senses**;

- **Water** that is the primordial Chaos, is fluidity and flexibility, and symbolizes your **subconscious mind**; **Intuition** is a deeper perception. Without clear evidence or proof, intuition perceives the subtle inner relationships and underlying processes creatively, and imaginatively.

- **Fire** that is boundless and invisible, and is a parching heat that consumes all, or within its highest manifestation, becomes the expression of Divine Love. It is a **symbol of your emotions**, and

- **Air** that has no shape and is incapable of any fixed form. It symbolizes **your world of thoughts**. It is a rational, systematic process, it is our intellectual comprehension of things.

All elements are bound by:

- **Soul** that stands at the center of the four elements as an Essence, an Observer, Consciousness coming forth to **experience the magic of Life**.

We will follow ancient philosophies: Taoists with their concept of Yin and Yang, Yogis with their belief in two opposite energy forces that flow through our body (Ida and Pingala), Jung that arranges the four functions (intuition, thinking, emotions, sensation) into two pairs of opposites – sensations / intuition and thinking / feeling that form our personality;

Your Highest Potential is Waiting

WE WILL NOT BE TALKING TO YOU ABOUT PARENTING BUT ABOUT HOW TO GROW AS A SPIRITUAL BEING TOGETHER WITH YOUR CHILDREN

Our intention is not to preach to you, to attack your ways of parenting, to blame you or highlight your mistakes, but to support you on your parenting journey, to inspire your higher self, to help you see and bring to consciousness the patterns that might hinder your growth.

Our intention is to help you constantly return to the energy of love no matter how much of a challenge parenting might be.

Our intention is to let you know that you are not alone in your parenting battle-field, within the arena of discomfort, sacrifice, and confusion that children might create and to help you see that your stage is surrounded with marvel, beauty, and plenty of unforgettable experiences.

The ancient truth is that no one can touch your buttons like your-own child can and no one can inspire within you so much owe, happiness, and wonder like your-own child.

We will try to help you potter each one of your and your children's days in such a way to create many moments of amazement.

We will help you at all time remember that you are a parent NOW and that this moment is unique and will never return.

Do not give up when you touch the door of awareness, frightened by its trap, but let it open wide giving your family a possibility to create reality of your dreams.

The main tools we will be using within Conscious Parenting course are:

Spiritual Journey Learn to Listen to Your Soul

Body Mind Soul

Train Love   Train Willpower

Respect Gaia   Respect Life

Respect Silence

Conscious Living

Mindful Eating   Mindful Being

Conscious Relationships

Mindfulness Training

We will help you look at:

- Your habits, stereotypical behaviors, prejudices
- Your dreams, & goals
- Listen to your Soul:
    - Learn Meditation & Mindfulness
    - Increasing Your capability to Love, Stay Inspired, Creative and Full of Energy
    - Using Your Soul's Diary & Spiritual Diary

Commitment Contract

Personal development **is never ending work.** It takes commitment and patience. If you are serious about personal growth, we will be more than happy to share what we know with you.

Commitment Contract

I _____

Undertake to work on my self-development during the next 12 weeks.

I commit to honestly and truthfully face my habits and beliefs, so that I can transform them into inspiring and enriching daily routines, and life-changing attitudes.

My intention is to discover and live my highest potential working with my body, mind and soul.

During these 12 weeks I commit to take care of my body giving it the adequate sleep, proper diet, and exercise. I will do my best to limit or avoid consumption of alcohol, drugs, cigarettes, and medications for the duration of the course.

I also commit to listen to my Soul's Whispers exercising daily meditation, writing Spiritual Diary, and creating my-own rituals for accessing the Power of Soul (contact with nature, music, dance, laughter, etc.).

I commit to experimenting, enjoying and exploring! Let my Soul and Mind stay Inspired!

_____ (signature)

_____ (date)

Rules of the Game

Listen to Each Other

    Speak One by One No Interruption Right to Disagree

    Respect One Another

        All Ideas are Good

            Questioning is Healthy

      There are no Stupid Answers or Opinions

            No Aggression

      Do not Judge

     Speak in Your own Name

    Be Honest, Truthful, and Thoughtful

           Listen Attentively and Practice

      Silence Win Win Scenario is The Best

  Switch Off Your Mobile Phones

When in Doubt, Ask Questions

  Be Conscious of Words You Use

Add your own Rule 1 _____

Rule 2 _____

    Rule 3 _____

Rule 4 _____

Conscious Parenting Main Principles

The main principles of **Conscious Parenting** are based around 3 pillars:

- **Love**
    - **Train Love**
    - **Practice Freedom**
    - **Be Mindful**
- **Rhythm**
    - **Create Stability**
    - **Respect Routine**
    - **Build Structure**
- **Priorities**
    - **Learn to Discriminate**
    - **Define Priorities**
    - **Practice Self-discipline to Execute**

Through this process will help you further develop: Awareness of many stereotypes that cover your path and hinder your thinking process

- Open heart that is protected by inner strength,
- Open and **Free Mind** so that you can stay in-tuned with your soul, new experiences and ideas,
- An ability to stay true to your decisions and do your best to follow them.

Remember, this is your Journey, your course and your Life. We will inspire you and offer you various tools and techniques for your Spiritual Growth but you will most benefit if you give yourself fully to It.

Conscious Parenting

'If we do not respect our **Earth**, the **World of Emotions** & Mental development will suffer. We all need **Rhythm** in our food consumption, sleep patterns, cleanliness & exercise regime. **This Routine does not come naturally** and it is learned and exercised from very young age.'

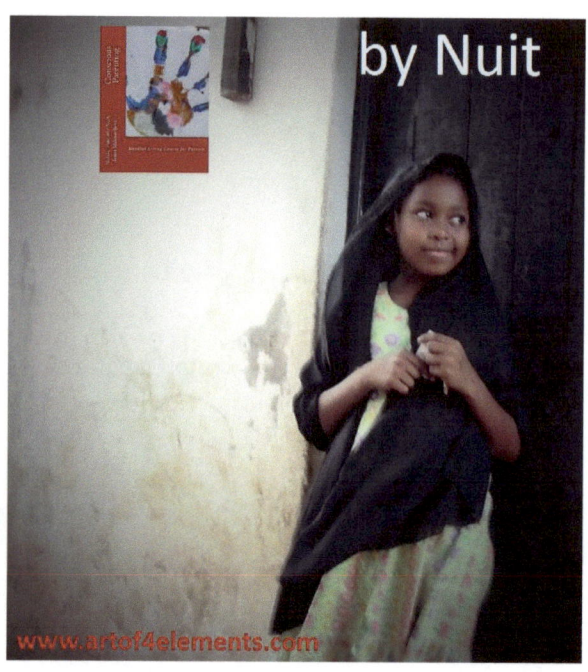

"The need for imagination, a sense of truth and a feeling of responsibility – these are the three forces which are the very nerve of education." **Rudolf Steiner**

Within the Artof4Elements Conscious Parenting Course Methodology, at all times, we are very attentive and careful about the child's evolving **world of senses** that needs stability**, routine, and structure**, that needs constant attention and care, **world of emotions** that needs **love, freedom and creativity** and **world of thoughts** that needs **Discrimination as an Ability to chose Right Thinking, Emotions, Behavior.**

Soul stands at the center of the children growth and development, as an Essence, an Observer, Consciousness coming forth to **experience the magic of Life.** Be tentative to the Soul's whispers.

A child has a deep longing to discover that the world is based on truth. Respect that longing. In our attempt to help children grow into inspired adults, we wish them to carry the youthfulness of their souls, and the wonders of childhood into their old age.

Listen to Your Child

A child is a Soul, a unit Consciousness materialized on Earth to learn, fulfill its purpose and contribute within the matrix of society. Our parents and grandparents fought for 'freedom', 'expression of thoughts', 'equality', and we now have a task to fight for the supremacy of Love over Control within all areas of life. An ocean of human consciousness and sub-consciousness is vast and dynamic. It beautifully changes with every enlightened human being that walks the planet, with every enlightened couple that lives love and with every enlightened parent that can transfer the wisdom to his or her little ones.

Stepping into the foot-steps of our ancestors, dreaming a better world we walk our path fighting for the mental, emotional and spiritual freedom, and equality.

Every child is an individual with a different growth rate and a potential that is varied and vast.

Respecting the needs of our little ones from a very early age, listening to their unique voices, hearing their wants will assure them that no matter how tiny they are somebody will kneel down to Listen.

Respecting the potential that is hidden within each child, we respect their potential to become Kings of their Trade, or Saviors of the World to come.

Kahlil Gibran on Children

'And a woman who held a babe against her bosom said, 'Speak to us of Children.' And he said:

Your children are not your children.

They are the sons and daughters of Life's longing for itself.

They come through you but not from you,

And though they are with you, yet they belong not to you.

You may give them your love but not your thoughts.

For they have their own thoughts.

You may house their bodies but not their souls,

For their souls dwell in the house of tomorrow, which you cannot visit, not even in your dreams.

You may strive to be like them, but seek not to make them like you.

For life goes not backward nor tarries with yesterday.

You are the bows from which your children as living arrows are sent forth.

The archer sees the mark upon the path of the infinite, and He bends you with His might that His arrows may go swift and far.

Let your bending in the archer's hand be for gladness;

For even as he loves the arrow that flies, so He loves also the bow that is stable.'

Rhythm

RHYTHM IS ONE OF THREE PILLARS OF CONSCIOUS PARENTING

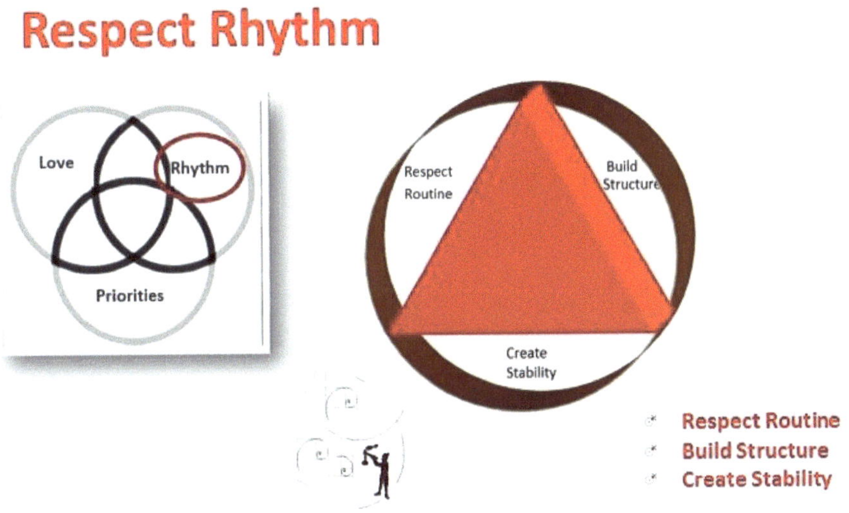

Respect Rhythm

- **Respect Routine**
- **Build Structure**
- **Create Stability**

RHYTHM IS BASIS OF ALL

If we do not respect our **Earth**, the world of emotions and mental development will suffer. We all need **rhythm** in our food consumption, in our sleep patterns, in our cleanliness and our exercise regime. This routine does not come naturally and it is learned and exercised from very young age.

The Rhythm is carried and supported by our ability to:

- **Respect Routine**
- **Create Stability**
- **Build Structure**

THE KIDS NEED RHYTHM, THEY NEED STABILITY, ROUTINE, STRUCTURE

Without the **routine** our body will suffer. It is a carefully structured activity and should be rigorously followed. The routine includes:

- Regular bed time, regular meal time, regular washing time, a set time for silence, a set time for creativity, a set time for play.

- The routine around food: at a set time, and place

- The routine around 'spaces': dinning at the dinning table, playing in the playing room, doing the home-work after school, etc.

How long do I, my partner or my child spend sleeping, eating, exercising?

If we wish to have a beautiful, peaceful and safe home, we need healthy expanding roots that go deep into the ground. These roots are our routine, our stability, our structure.

Conscious Parenting
by Nuit

'To chose **Happiness** as a way of life, we need to learn to **Love** and children are our best teachers, we need to learn to **Concentrate** and to **teach our children** the **Magic of Concentration**, and no matter how difficult this sounds, we should keep the **steady flow of inspiration** within our lives.'

www.artof4elements.com

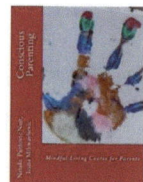

The life with the **rhythm** will give us space and time for all the other activities. The life with the stability, structure and routine will give us time for ourselves, our children, cousins, friends, work, study, theater, for all…

The rhythm is a movement and a flow. The flow can be expanding or directed from one side to the other. The directed flow secures predictability and stability to your family and your kids.

Even if they do not define it as such, children love when they are stable and secure.

> **Socrates** about the youth of his time: "Our youth now love luxury. They have bad manners, contempt for authority; they show disrespect for their elders and love chatter in place of exercise; they no longer rise when elders enter the room; they contradict their parents, chatter before company; gobble up their food and tyrannize their teachers."

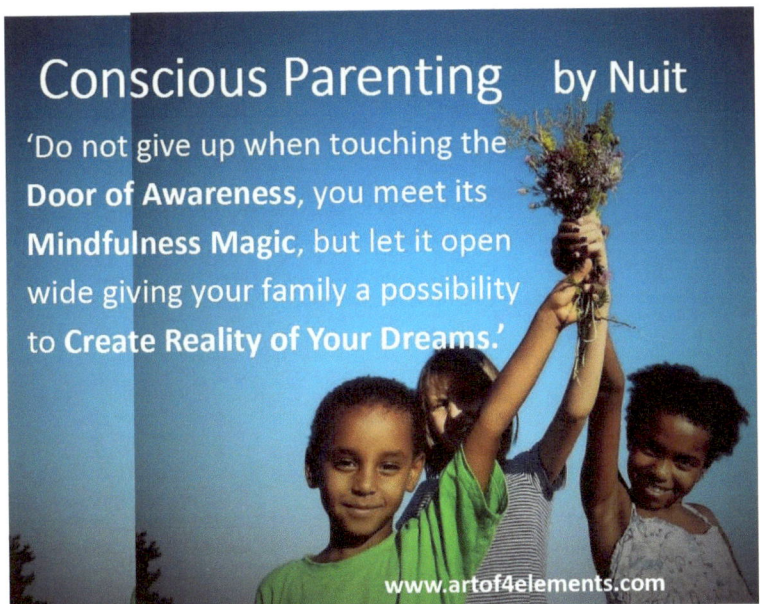

Respect Routine, Create Stability, Build Structure

The children like to know that they will go for an outing with the family on Sunday morning and that this Sunday morning will happen no matter what. They also like to know that they will be fed properly daily and that you will together bake pancakes every Thursday afternoon. They like to know that they will play with their friends once they finish their homework and that they will return home for a warm home-made meal in the evening. They like to know that you will read to them before they go to sleep and that they will feed the cat first thing in the morning.

Tt is not easy to find the rhythm in today's world full of various destructions, and it is not easy to find 'time' when so much is spent in useless activities (TV and computers) but it is possible to do so, and if you manage your child will start thriving.

Routine and **structure** will build **stability** and help you and your children gain a healthy attitude towards food, build positive habits, and know when to be active and when to withdraw.

It is often that children have problems expressing themselves within the families that find it difficult to connect with the rhythm and structure as a quality. Their parents find the rhythm boring and the structure suffocating and are incapable of planning their activities in advance. They allow other people to shape their day and they jump from an activity to the other, without any respect for their own needs for the rhythm and structure. This reflects on the children. One of the reasons for AD/HD problem in early childhood is the luck of rhythm and structure.

Rhythm has a flow and like a river it carries us throughout the day. It is important for both us and our children that this flow is steady and **stable**, that we are sailing through the day peacefully, not jumping from an activity to the other, or staying 'dead' tired with no movement / activities / stimuli. If we allow within our structure time for stillness and time for play, we will balance the two and enjoy them both.

Rhythm is everywhere, in nature, in seasons, it is constant and it changes at all times. The rhythm is within our body, within our breathing, heart beat, and menstrual cycles. The newborn has its-own rhythm of sleeping, eating, being. We are at all times surrounded with the rhythm and we at all times follow the **rhythms**.

PRIORITIES

PRIORITIES IS ONE OF THREE PILLARS OF CONSCIOUS PARENTING

Define Priorities

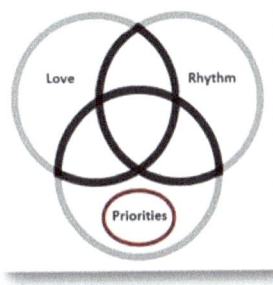
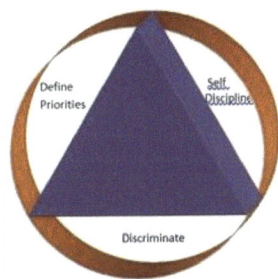

- **Learn to Discriminate**
- **Define Priorities**
- **Practice Self-Discipline & Execute**

PRIORITIES ARE BUILT AND SUPPORTED BY OUR ABILITY TO:

- **Learn to Discriminate**
- **Define Priorities**
- **Practice Self-Discipline to Execute**

Defining **Priorities** and exercising **Self-discipline** will help you grow as a **conscious parent**, help you get better organized and your happiness will multiply. When we plan our day, that doesn't mean that we will constantly 'run around' the clock and live like solders, but it means that we will slowly, step by step, bring our house in order.

YOUR CIRCLE OF LIFE

For you to understand the magic of prioritizing we will start with a practical exercises that gives you an insight about your own life...

YOUR CIRCLE OF 24 HOURS ACTIVITIES

Draw the circle of your activities during 24 hours.

If you think that you can remember, draw the circle of your activities immediately. But if in any doubt, just spend a day observing yourself: how much time did I watch TV, spend on Facebook, play Games, sleep, eat, play?

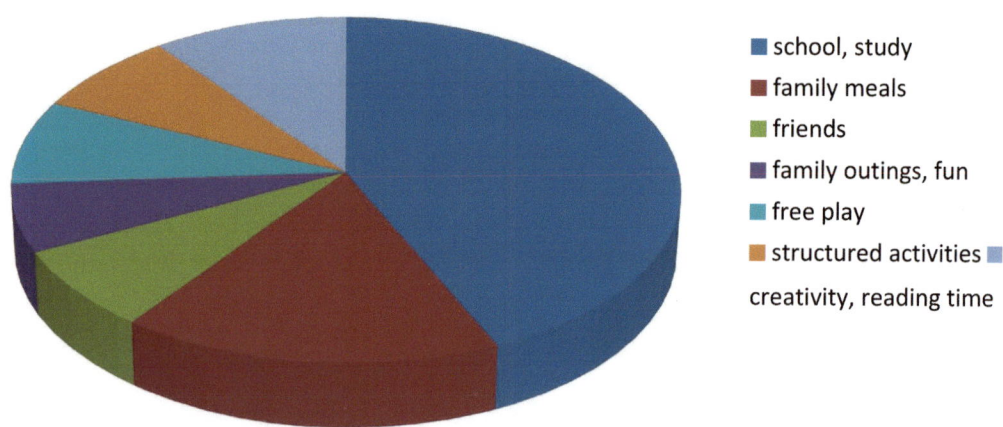

Now, analyze the list. Analyze your chart.

Take a colorful marker and highlight areas that you need to protect, activities that just MUST take place, so that you restore your inner happiness.

Draw the circle of your kids' activities during 24 hours.

Our suggestion for the 24 hours circle of life for your children could include:

1. Rhythm around food, body cleanliness, sleep and exercise
2. Time to be tender: a hug, a kiss, a cures, 'tickling time' with your child, with your partner, with your loved ones
3. Time to be alone, time to be silent. Children will also learn to respect the time for silence. Practice silence with them. Your silent time, could become their reading time, diary time, music time or drawing time.
4. Time to be with friends, pets, plants. Time with your pets, time tending the flowers
5. Family time: cooking, beading, playing, talking, walking
6. Reading time, learning time, music time, art time
7. Free time / free play

When you look at your day, observe the time you've spent on your own, the time you spent with your partner, with your children alone, the time you spent with your friends, and the time you spent with strangers. Create the balance within these activities, the balance of your relationships interactions.

THERE SHOULD BE A SUBTLE BALANCE BETWEEN TIME SPENT INDOORS AND TIME SPENT OUTDOORS

THERE SHOULD BE A BALANCE BETWEEN TIME SPENT ALONE AND TIME SPENT WITH FRIENDS

THERE SHOULD EXIST A BALANCE AROUND TIME SPENT IN A STRUCTURED ACTIVITY AND TIME SPENT IN FREE PLAY

AREAS TO PROTECT

Areas to Protect:	Me	My Partner	My Child
Family Meal	√		
Creativity Time	√		√
Free Play, Free Time			√
Study Time			
Friends Time			
Silent Time or Time on my own		√	
Quality Time with my Partner, Kids	√	√	√

In the evening the next day, write down your protected areas and how did you take care of them today:

- Did you skip a meal?
- Did you eat on the go?
- Did you have time for art and music?
- Did you go for your daily walk?
- Did you forget to do something that you have promised to yourself ages ago?

If you have, write down briefly what are you going to do tomorrow, what are you going to do better, what are you going to do different?

Have in mind that children will not help you with the rhythm, they will try to break it apart, it is you who needs to train it and implement it within your lives.

Your Circle of Activities during 1 week

Draw the circle of your activities during 1 week.

Do the circle of activities for all the members of the family. It will be interesting to get an insight of the mother's activities, of the father's activities and of the children's activities.

- ♥ Time to work / go to school
- ♥ Time for house chores: washing clothes, cleaning the house
- ♥ Time to rest / be together as a family
- ♥ Structured time for various activities (basketball, music lessons, sport)
- ♥ Free time for unstructured activities.
- ♥ Time for art and music (crafts morning, music afternoon, theater evening)
- ♥ Time for friends (one or two days for meeting friends)
- ♥ Time for the family activity (family outing) with friends
- ♥ Time for the family activity (family outing) without friends

Observe and analyze Your Charts

Do not clutter your children time with too many activities.

Activity after activity can cause hyperactivity with children and it will be very tiring for grown-ups. Allow some free and breathing time during your week.

For example: every second day there should be a 'breathing' space of no structured activities. If you think that this is impossible, create your schedule in such a way that one day is spent with the father, one day with the mother, one day planned so that the whole family is together.

Be conscious of how many times you leave your kids with strangers to take care of them so that you will go to work or get some rest. They already spend a lot of time with strangers at school, so they probably need you and your time with them, as suppose to running around from one to the other after school activity.

This is especially important when your child is less than 4 years old. Waldorf schools do not accept children that are less than 4 years old for that reason, they believe that children of that age should be with their parents.

Monday	SCHOOL			FAMILY DINNER	
Tuesday	SCHOOL		BASKETBALL	FAMILY DINNER	IN BED BY 8:00
Wednesday	SCHOOL	LUNCH OUT WITH KIDS	MUSIC LESSON	FAMILY DINNER	
Thursday	SCHOOL			FAMILY DINNER	
Friday	SCHOOL		COMPUTER TIME, GAMES, OR A FILM	FAMILY DINNER	
Saturday	BASKETBALL	MUSIC LESSON	FRIENDS	FAMILY DINNER	EVENING OUT
Sunday	FAMILY DAY		PLAY IN THE PARK	FAMILY DINNER	

Stop in Wonder! Your Life is Passing Un-noticed

Your Family Events Circle of Activities during 1 Month

Draw the circle of your family related activities during 1 month

- Theater at least once a month
- Family outings without friends at least 4 times a month
- Family outings with friends at least 4 times a month
- Inviting friends over at least twice a month
- Spend time in nature etc.

Your Family Events Circle of Activities during 1 year

Examples include:

- A Family holiday with at least 10 days away spent together
- Christmas preparation day, Eastern preparation day, Halloween preparation day, Carnival day, Birthdays Party of each one of the family member
- Birthday Parties
- Once or twice a year, write a love letter to the other member of your family
- Make a surprise party for a member of the family or a friend.
- Creative ideas together: Write a play, a pantomime, a song and perform it with your children.

Observe the Charts. Is there anything that you can learn from them? Observe

the time wasters, become conscious of them.

- How much time do you spend watching TV, on the computer, playing games?
- Do you have enough time on your own?
- Do you have enough creative time?
- Do you spend enough time with friends?

DRAW THE CIRCLE OF ACTIVITIES WITHIN YOUR IDEAL LIFE

Within the circle, you can include anything that inspires you that makes you feel good, that you aspire to. Don't forget to include the following areas:

- Your healthy body including proper rest, exercise, preparation of healthy food, etc.
- An area that says friends, and relationship with friends;
- Time spent with your loved ones: partner, parents, sister, etc.
- An area with your ideal work;
- Meditation, walks, dance, poetry, reading, your spiritual methods and tools (meditation, prayer, etc.)
- An area for pleasure, travel and adventure.

Look at it and meditate on it. This pie will later help you define goals within your life.

Siva Vaidhyanadhan

'Real education happens only by failing, changing, challenging, and adjusting. All of those gerunds apply to teachers as well as students. No person is an "educator," because education is not something one person does to another. Education is an imprecise process, a dance, and a collaborative experience.'

Love

Practice Love

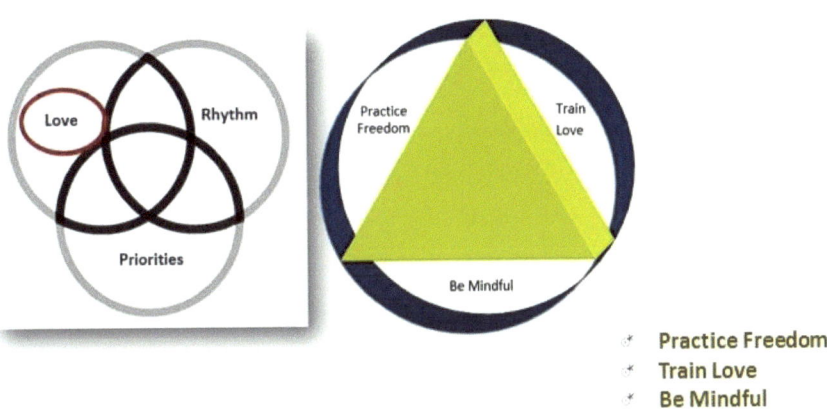

- Practice Freedom
- Train Love
- Be Mindful

LOVE IS ONE OF THREE PILLARS OF CONSCIOUS PARENTING THE

ENERGY OF LOVE EXPANDS WITH OUR ABILITY TO:

- **Train Love**
- **Practice Freedom**
- **Be Mindful**

Showing our little ones how to express love, we teach them emotional intelligence, we teach them to express, to recognize what is happening within them, and to live within their reach and expanding world of emotions.

Stop the world turning, stop your child, go onto your knees and look at your little one in the eyes, pick it up, give it a cures, a hug, a kiss, stop and say your child 'I love you'.

It is important to get out of the role of the 'mother' that constantly directs, controls, orders, and to come back to love that is the main natural flow between you and your child.

TRAIN LOVE

MEDITATE ABOUT LOVE

Think about the quality of love in relation to your life

Ask yourself a question:

WHEN DO I EXERCISE LOVE IN THE BEST POSSIBLE WAY?

For example: I can express love in the best way when:

- I honor my Self
- I am relaxed
- I am playful
- I know what I want
- When I am aware of the situation, surroundings and causes and effects. Awareness guides me through this matrix of karmic influences, subconscious chains, and invisible lies to the understanding of True Self.

The first encounter with a child's emotional make-up is fascinating. Children scream at all times, shout, and impulsively hit all around them. Often they complain about their surroundings. **We are quite frightened of children and we do our best to 'tie' them, to 'obstruct' them, to 'control' them.**

We have invented push-chairs to help us carry them, but children feel safest around their parents, listening to their heart-beat, and breathing with them. We have invented cots to separate the little ones from us while we are sleeping, but this scenario is very 'un-natural' for the new-borns. All the other animals keep their babies around them at that tender age. We invented baby-chairs and we tie them to the chairs while they are eating, instead of holding them in our arms and sharing food with them.

Children need to feel our **love** at all times, our **love** gives them confidence that they are heard, that they are present, and that they matter. A warm, loving and gentle environment is absorbed unconsciously and it gives children a wonderful start to life.

Children perceive our emotions and map them, so if we are angry, they will be frightened or chaotic.

- Carry your child, sleep with your child, do not tie your child down

- Play with your child. Invent stories for your child, and let your child invent stories for you

- Listen to your child. There is something s/he is trying to tell you with his/her screams

- Do not let your child get lost in the world of TV, computers, games, let him/her explore nature instead.

We are the first one to teach our children love and how to express it within the relationship with other human beings, with animals, with nature. If we teach our boy not to cry because he is a boy, we will teach him how to get a liver failure later on in life, because he will not be capable to express and live his emotions properly. This amazing world of emotional intelligence will help him or her clearly communicate his likes and dislikes later on in life.

So, WHEN DO YOU EXERCISE LOVE IN THE BEST POSSIBLE WAY?

Once we learn how to abandon negative thoughts and feelings, polishing the mirror of our mind through meditation, and training of virtues, through living Love for all, the light from within becomes our reality.

Discovering the Philosopher's Stone within, becoming a child once more, living Love every single day, are all the keys to this amazing door to Happiness.

A-Ma Alchemy of Love by Nuit

'Any substance, an **Alchemist** would tell you, is what it appears to be, set just for **a moment lost in eternity**, by parameters of a given **place, time**, and circumstances.

When **one** is treated with **love**, **respect** and **care**, how far can he develop?'

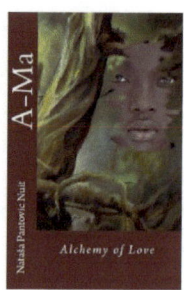

www.artof4elements.com

EXERCISE FREEDOM

Exploring, experiencing and imitating the world of grown-us through free play, children are given a chance to unconsciously learn and emotionally mature through their own games.

Too much of today's learning is structured, children are 'directed', 'instructed' and carefully 'followed' at all times, so they do not have a chance to experience learning through unobstructed observation.

Children have **deep devotion to life** and this devotion is beautifully expressed through the **free play**. Objects of play should be as simple as possible, to allow the power of imagination to flourish. Buying 'perfect', expensive toys, rob the children of an ability to see beauty in a stone or a shell.

Freedom should be an integral ingredient of your child's growth. **Children** learn **intuitively**, perceiving the subtle inner relationships observing nature. Free creative play is an invaluable gift that children need to start properly relating to the outside world.

Children first learn through **experimenting**, and the fascinating world around them, of flowers, animals, stones, has so much to offer, so there is no need to rush their thinking process / development. Once the thinking starts, it should be treated as the most fascinated activity completely supported with the world of images and emotions.

- Spend time in nature or go to a park and let your child play. Try not to interfere in the activity of the play. Let the child discover, explore, invent the objects of play.
- Children also learn beautifully when with other children. They learn not to scream, shout or hit, because other children at all times challenge their emotional make-up.

BE MINDFUL

Mindfulness works with continuous awareness of body, breath; feelings, thoughts, intentions. Our state of mind, our positive or negative attitude towards the world, is closely related to our experiences of happiness or suffering. Mindfulness is awareness of everything that is happening in the moment of 'Now'. Mindfulness is a self development technique that will change the focus of our mind towards happiness.

Mindfulness is continuous undisturbed awareness of the present moment. Fully aware of here, and now, we pay attention to what is happening right in front of us, we set aside our mental and emotional baggage. To be mindful we have to re-train our mind.

Our mind is constantly busy with thoughts and feeling about our past, present and future. To stop it from useless constant chat, we must learn how to hear this noise, how to become aware of it, and to transform it through concentration into mindfulness.

We train ourselves all through our life to waste energy following our inner narratives. We are often unconsciously driven by our fears, worries and fantasies. We interpret, speculate, and project the words, thoughts and emotions around us. We should enter a space of awareness of our present moment with no emotional filters, no regrets of the past or hopes for the future, with no daydreaming and no nightmares. An ability to concentrate will give us an ability to transform a mundane situation into a very special one.

With 70,000 thoughts a day and 95% of our activity controlled by the subconscious mind, no wonder that it feels as though we are asleep most of the time. To awake, we need to train self-remembering and mindfulness. Self-remembering is an attempt to be more conscious, and more aware. It is a form of active meditation were we work to be aware of ourselves and our environment through self-remembering. The essence of the Self-Remembering technique is that while we are doing anything: reading, singing, talking, tasting, we must be aware of the Self who is reading, singing, talking or tasting.

Mindfulness increases the awareness of the nature of the mind. If we learn to control our mind and listen to our souls we can consciously choose to be joyful instead of sad, peaceful and loving, alert and relaxed...

Being mindful of our feelings we will get Delighted. The quality of life is in proportion of our capacity to get delighted. The capacity for delight is within our capacity to pay attention to things around us. Pay attention to birds singing, to clouds formations, to flowers greeting you, to kids laughing, to a beautiful person that have just passed by. Be aware of synchronicity among all living beings and be alert for the presence of Divine in All.

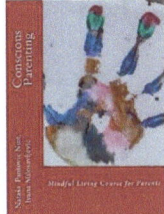

Children **love learning through rhymes**, they **love poetry**, painting, **story-telling**, cooking, knitting, and their thinking capability beautifully develops supported by music, arts, and sports. The development of thoughts should go hand in hand with the development of feelings and heart.

At the age of 7 to 14, our children are learning to have a beautiful **capacity for feelings** that will give them a rich soul experiences, and they are expressing a wonderful hunger for knowledge for Philosophia (love of wisdom). It is **love** and **wisdom** that are the two greatest gifts of mankind.

The children's imagination is a feeling force. Respect the world of images, avoid abstract and bloodless thoughts. Sarcasm can be most hurtful and destructive force

- **Use music, dance and painting** as tools for inner expression

- Allow your child to cook, wash dishes, take care of plants, take care of animals. These activities are extremely interesting and fulfilling.

Conscious Parenting by Nuit

Practice **Focus with Love** with your kids and they will approach every single task with **Focus** and **Love**. To be able to exercise 'focus' in day-to-day life, a child should have **time to relax, time for silence, time to perfect activities**, time to **focus** & **wonder**.

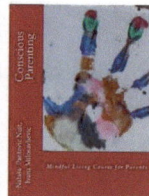

What is Unconditional Love?

Love and Happiness

The essence of this wonderful feeling, this joyful state of being is that Love can and must be trained! To choose Happiness as the way of Life, one needs to train Love The Soul that chose the path of developing the virtues becomes intoxicated with good qualities, and it starts fully and deeply loving and trusting, living within this space of openness, living within the space of Being Love.

Falling in Love

Professor Arthur Arun, the New York psychologist, studied the dynamics of what happens when people fall in love and within his experiment he asked complete strangers to spend around half an hour together, to share intimate details of their lives with each other, and they were asked to stare into each others eyes for a few minutes, silently. As a result of this experiment, many couples reported that they felt a strong attraction / falling in love for each other and two of them even got married.

What is Love?

So, what do you think? **What is love**? If we enter the space of **openness** and **trust**, can we **fall in love** with a complete stranger? If you have experienced love, you will agree with me that being loved and loving fills us with a warm, secure, floating feeling. **Living love**, we start listening to our inner-most being, and we chose to be happy.. Touched by the Love Magic we open, and dissolve our boundaries. However, the Cupid's arrow also carries jealousy, it exposes us to our ugly side, working with our sub-consciousness fears...

Our philosophers, our poets, our scientists, tell us that the formula of our Universe is Love, governed by Venus. She combines the highest spiritual with the lowest material qualities - Love materialised on Earth. She is born in water, from mud, and she bears the lotus. Her mystical mantra is: 'Love is the law, but Love controlled by Will'.

LOVE NEEDS TO BECOME A CONSCIOUS EFFORT, LOVE NEEDS TO BE TRAINED

The love parents feel for their children, the love between partners, the love for friends are all wonderful exercises for worshipers of Love. When in love, we have a tendency to exaggerate small positive qualities or not to see negative ones, getting disappointed when we 'fall-out' of love and open our eyes to all the partner's vices. Love needs to enter our daily meditations, become our guide, and become part of our being.

Mindful Being
by Nuit

'Our philosophers, our poets, our scientists, tell us that the **Formula of our Universe is Love** governed by **Venus**. She combines the **highest spiritual** with the **lowest material** qualities: **Love** materialised on **Earth**. She is born in water, from mud, & she bears the lotus. Her **mystical mantra** is: **'Love is the Law, but Love controlled by Will'**.

www.artof4elements.com

UNCONDITIONAL LOVE

'No matter how new the face or how different the dress and behavior, there is no significant division between us and other people. It is foolish to dwell on external differences, because our basic natures are the same. Ultimately, humanity is one and this small planet is our only home, If we are to protect this home of ours, each of us needs to experience a vivid sense of universal altruism. It is only this feeling that can remove the self-centered motives that cause people to deceive and misuse one another.' **Dalai Lama**

Transformation tools, Conscious Parenting

MODULE 1 BODY

Module 1: We will help you examine your body, your health, the food that you eat, your habits and patterns.

Our purpose is **to help you grow as a *Conscious Human Being*.**

OBSERVE YOUR NUTRITION

We highly recommend that you spend the first 4 days in measuring your time spent in exercising, resting, and observing your eating and drinking habits. We are often too tired to consciously observe our eating and drinking patents. Also we often do not remember the truth and we need to make a conscious effort to record our habits so that we can become aware of them. We included only you and your child / children. It is the best if your partner is also following the program so that you can inspire each other and grow together.

DAY 1 TO 4 LET'S LOOK AT YOUR DRINKING HABITS

Observe your habits and the habits of your children in respect to drinking. Take a notebook with you and jot down all the liquids that you in-take during the first four days. Do not consciously or sub-consciously obstruct your usual habits. This exercise is designed to raise your awareness around drinking.

Day 1 to 4	Your Drinking Habits	Day 1		Quality (1-5)	Quantity (1-5)
	Drinking water	IIII		3	3
	Drinking juices				
	Drinking non caffeinated tea	3	Day 2 - Day 3 - Day 4		
	Drinking caffeinated tea	1			
	Hot chocolate, milk-shake, etc.				
	Drinking coffee	1			
	Wine, beer, liquids,	1			
	Other			3	3

Note: I is 1 unit: 2dl of water, 1 cup of tea, 1 espresso, 1dl of wine, etc

WORK WITH THE SAME TABLE TO HIGHLIGHT DRINKING HABITS OF YOUR CHILD

CONSCIOUS PARENTING COURSE   MODULE 1 MINDFUL EATING   OBSERVATION EXERCISE 1

Date_____   Name_____

Your Drinking Habits	Day 1	Day 2/3/4	Quality (1-5)	Quantity (1-5)
Water				
Milk				
Freshly squeezed fresh fruit, veggies				
Herbal non caffeinated tea				
Caffeinated tea				
Packed juices or fizzy drinks				
Hot chocolate, milk-shake, etc.				
Wine, beer, liquids				
Other				

Note: I is 1 unit: 2dl of water, 1 cup of tea, 1 espresso, 1dl of wine, etc

Your Notes:

DAY 1 TO 4 LET'S LOOK AT YOUR **EATING HABITS**

Observe your food habits. Take a note-book with you and jot down all the food items that you in-take during the day. Do not consciously or sub-consciously obstruct your usual habits. This exercise is designed to raise your awareness around eating.

Day 1 to 4	Your Eating Habits	Day 1	Day 2-4	Quality (1-5)	Quantity (1-5)
	Breakfast (quality)	- muesli - fruit - yogurt		Your mark for quality	Your mark for quantity
	Lunch		- toast & salad		
	Dinner	- rice - veggies			
	Snaking		- crisp - croissant		
	Over-eating	Y dinner			
	Fresh Fruit	1 apple			
	Fresh Vegetables	Veggie Soup			
	Organic	(Y/N) ✔			
	Seasonal, Local	(Y/N) ✔			
	Frozen, Can Ready made,	(Y/N)			
	Junk Food	- chips			
	Hidden sugars food	- coke (7 spoons)			
	Sweets	- 1 cake			
	Do you sit down to eat	(Y/N)			
	Restaurant / Home Made	HM			
	Carbohydrate overdose	(Y/N) ✔			
	Meat overdose	(Y/N) ✔			

Conscious Parenting Course   Module 1 Mindful Eating   Observation Exercise 2

Date_____   Name_____

Your Eating Habits	Day 1	Day 2	Qlty (1-5)	Qnty (1-5)
Breakfast				
Lunch				
Dinner				
Snaking				
Over-eating				
Fresh Fruit				
Fresh Veggies				
Organic				
Seasonal, Local				
Frozen, Canned				
Junk Food				
Hidden sugars				
Sweets, obvious sugars				
Sit down to eat				
Restaurant or Home Made				
Carbohydrate overdose				
Meat overdose				

Your Notes:

WORK WITH THE SAME TABLE TO HIGHLIGHT EATING HABITS OF YOUR CHILD

At the end of your observation, you will be able to produce the following table for both yourself and your child:

Balanced and healthy diet	Day 1	Day 2-4
I have a balanced and healthy diet, I eat lots of fresh greens and veggies		
My child has a balanced and healthy diet, s/he eats lots of fresh greens and veggies		
My partner has a balanced and healthy diet, eats lots of fresh greens and veggies		
I drink healthy, I take enough water and my water is of good quality		
My child's drinking patterns are healthy. S/he drinks enough water and his/her water is of good quality.		
My partner drinks healthy, taking enough water and water is of good quality		

At the end of the observation period, we will work with a questionnaire that highlights your habits, patterns, re-occurring problems.

Have in mind that this questionnaire is YOURS. Add any question that you feel is more relevant for your life. Be truthful and honest and your Soul will rejoice!

Personality Questionnaire 1 Your attitude towards your body

Answer the following Personality Questions: Your nutrition, health and body
Read each sentence and rate them from 1 (really bad) to 5 (I am super happy with it).

Answer to what extent you feel this statement is true.

My Body Questionnaire	1-2-3-4-5
I drink enough water and my water is of good quality	
I have a balanced and healthy diet, I eat lots of fresh greens and veggies	
I do not over-eat, I am happy with my weight	
My energy levels are high	
My sleep is of good quality and I am happy with its quantity	
I exercise regularly: I walk, roller-blade, swim, run at least three times per week	
My caffeine intake is healthy	
I rarely drink alcohol, use drugs, use medication, smoke	
I do not use sugars excessively / soft-drinks / food items loaded with sugar	
I do not eat junk food, use refined salt or food items loaded with salt	
I spend every day in Nature	
I spend enough time on-my-own meditating / contemplating / Being	

Write the answers of the Personality Questionnaire

After you have answered your questions, meditate on answers and where the problems within your life might be. Use a colored marker to highlight areas that might need improvement. Add whatever you feel is missed out from this list. The ranking from 1 to 5 will indicate your list of priorities.

Mindful Eating   by Nuit

Empower your **Physical Body**, helping your **Mind** and **Soul**:
1. Chose **Healthy Food**
2. Create **Daily Routine** with **Nutritional Habits**
3. Eat **Mindfully** practicing **Mindfulness & Willpower Exercises**

with Delicious RAW VEGAN RECIPES
www.artof4elements.com

My List of Priorities:
Items Marked as 1, 2 and 3 are:

My Body Questionnaire	1	2	3

EXERCISE 1 DEFINING YOUR AREAS FOR IMPROVEMENT

Study each answer that you are not happy with and determine what precise action you would like to do to change your state of body, mind, emotions.

Write down the areas that need improvement.

Be specific

For Example:

My Body feels depleted of energy			
Because of:	Action Items:	What stops you from doing it?	Any alternative?
My lousy posture	Do some Pilates to strengthen your spine	Hate Pilates	Try Yoga
My food allergies	Visit the doctor to determine the list of food	Hate doctors	Try alternative methods – muscle testing, etc.
A cough that won't leave	A doctor / A herbalist	My cough is not serious enough just annoying	More tea, care, lemon & honey, more rest
Not getting enough sleep	My bed is not firm enough	Never got to buying a new one	Let's do it than!

Often, we guess the solution of our problem but our habitual-mind-set invents a valid reason against the improvement. So that is why our list of action has a column called: Alternatives. There are always alternatives that will help your condition and are difficult to refuse.

CONSCIOUS PARENTING COURSE   MODULE 1 MINDFUL EATING   EXERCISE 1

Date_____   Name_____

Defining Areas of Improvement:

Because of:	Action Items:	What stops you from doing it?	Any alternative?

Write the action items that you would like to pursue, so that these conditions change.

Defining Areas of Improvement:

Action 1	Alternative Action	Time Frame	First Step towards the Action

EXERCISE 2 RHYTHM AND FOOD

If you have a problem with over-eating, eating too often, eating too little, eating junk food, food allergies, etc. you need to become aware and conscious of your body / mind reactions to food.

EXERCISE 2A RE-CREATE THE ROUTINE AROUND YOUR FOOD

- Eat around the table.
- Eat at set times.
- Eat with no distractions

We are all children that need **nurturing**, **love** and **care**. So give your inner child that nurturing and love, give yourself back the joy of preparing healthy and nutritious meals. Re-create the routine around your food: eat around the table, eat at the set times, don't skip your meals.

When you eat, just eat, do not do anything else. Do not read or watch news, use this time to become conscious of quality and quantity of food that you are taking. Your enjoyment will multiply and fulfillment soon follow. The quality will replace the quantity, **awareness** will become your guide and protector. Taste your healthy and nutritious meals without external interruptions, experience the joy of tasting food without TV, reading, working, rush, mobile, messaging, etc. Savor and enjoy your food while eating, become 'mindful' of your food, rather than just swallowing your food while watching TV, surfing the Net, or reading the paper.

Exercise 2B Chose your Food Mindfully

SWAP
- ☐ meat for veggies
- ☐ soft drinks for spring water (with a bit of lemon)
- ☐ packed & processed foods with organics
- ☐ sugar with honey or fruits
- ☐ milk-chocolate bar for a piece of dark chocolate
- ☐ a handful of sweets for a handful of berries
- ☐ an apple pie for a baked apple
- ☐ cream for plain yoghurt
- ☐ 2nd cup of coffee for a cup of white or green tea

www.artof4elements.com

- ❤ swap meat for veggies
- ❤ swap white for brown
- ❤ swap soft drinks for spring water (with a bit of lemon or lime)
- ❤ swap colored and processed food with organics
- ❤ swap sugar with honey or fruits
- ❤ swap a milk-chocolate bar for a piece of dark
- ❤ chocolate swap a handful of sweets for a handful of
- ❤ berries swap an apple pie for a baked apple swap
- ❤ cream for plain yogurt
- ❤ swap 2nd cup of coffee for a cup of white or green tea

Become conscious of quality and quantity of food that you are taking.

Let it be fresh, organic, locally grown, seasonal, nutritious, use non-processed wholemeal items, and lots of raw veggies. Let the quality of your food items replace the quantity, and allow the food awareness to become your guide.

With the awareness you will start respecting yourself and the enjoyment will multiply.

EAT LOTS OF FRUIT AND VEGGIES

Nothing else can replace or substitute **fruits and vegetable**s in our diet. Fruits and vegetables provide the body with our #1 source of antioxidants, vitamins and minerals.

Fruit have their **best healing and nutrition effects** when eaten separately from grains and vegetables. Eat fruits one hour before consuming any other foods and the best time is MORNING.

Maintaining good health requires balancing the alkaline and acidic level of your blood through your nutrition and your lifestyle choices. The way certain foods are chosen and prepared can change how healthy they are for us. Let it be fresh, healthy, without preservatives, suitable for you. Let it be tasty and looking wonderful.

Mindful Eating   by Nuit

We do food every single day. **Conscious Eating** is a big step toward **Conscious Living**. Quality and Quantity of Food is directly related to our **Health and State of Mind**. We can use food to help us **recover** from **Stress and Disease**. Not taking food seriously will eventually lead to Stress or Disease

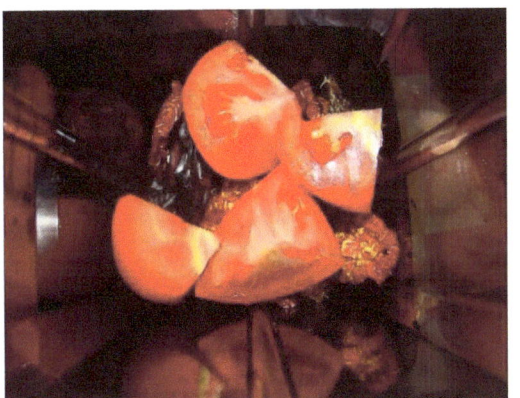

With Delicious RAW VEGAN RECIPES
www.artof4elements.com

Exercise 2C Eat Mindfully

Be aware of that sensation of chewing and somewhere in the middle of the bite, stop for a moment, to again experience the battle of senses that occurs when we are eating.

1. Decorate Your Table

Preparing food could be an art form, a very beautiful one! So, decorate your table. Arrange your food using your nicest plates, light a candle and place a flower arrangement on your table as though you are serving a guest!

2. Start eating after a short meditation or prayer

This will make you face the animal instinct of HUNGER, and you will turn again towards Peace.

Just before you take your first bite, sit in front of your food for a minute or two before eating. You may wish to close your eyes. Respecting the food, the space around you, the silence, will make you face your animal instinct of HUNGER, relax you, and you will turn towards food peacefully.

3. **Stay with this instinct to swallow**

Keep the food in your mouth for some time and observe the instinct to take more than it is really necessary, to gulp the food. We are practicing **awareness**. We want the process of food consumption to enter into our **awareness**.

We want to be aware of what we are eating, aware of our addictions, aware of our animal instincts. When under the light of consciousness these instincts become weaker and we can use them for more pleasure, instead of suffering within our sense of greed.

4. **Eat Your Meal Mindfully**

Eat slowly, chew properly, lift your fork gradually and thoughtfully, experiencing every movement fully. After finishing your meal, take a few moments to notice that you have finished.

Allow the feeling of gratitude to fill your mind, you just had this wonderful nourishing meal to support you on your further journey.

5. **Stop eating just before you are full**

If we over-eat, we feel drowsy, we are not fully active, If we leave the table a little hungry, we feel much more energized later on.

6. **Taste a wide range of food items**

Try sweet and sour foods, liquids and solids, hot and cold foods. Before you eat, smell your food, as though you are experiencing the finest wine, stay with each experience.

7. **Enjoy Your Meal!**

Mindful Eating   by Nuit

Real Food is not GMO modified, has no poisons, no preservatives, no coloring's **Real Food** is **Fruit** and **Veggies** that are seasonal & local. **Real Food** is **not processed, frozen, or prep-packaged** Whole, unprocessed foods are much healthier.

with Delicious RAW VEGAN RECIPES
www.artof4elements.com

EXERCISE 3 CREATE YOUR DREAM HEALTHY MENU

EXERCISES FOR RAISING AWARENESS AROUND FOOD: HEALTHY VEGETARIAN MEAL PLAN

Create your-own healthy vegetarian meal plan for a week. Try it out for a week!

An example of a healthy vegetarian meal plan would look like this:

	Breakfast	Lunch	Snacks	Dinner
Monday	Quinoa with Strawberries, Coconut, Seeds	Spinach and Greens Salad	Popcorns	Whole Wheat Vegetable Stuffed Flatbread
Tuesday	Buckwheat Pancakes with fruits and nuts	Raw experiment: Sprouts, tomato, avocado, carrots	Fresh Seasonal Fruit + Pumpkin Seeds	Crackers with Hummus and Veggies
Wednesday	Coconut millet	Feta and Avocado Wraps	Blackberries and Walnuts	Whole Wheat Pancakes (See: Unhealthy Treats)
Thursday	Fruit feast + Green Smoothie	Roasted Vegetables with Cheese Sauce	Yogurt	Pasta with Pesto
Friday	Raw Buckwheat Porridge	See: Lunch Out	Brown Toast with Honey	Roasted Veggies and Rice

Conscious Parenting Module 1 Mindful Eating Exercise 3 Dream Menu

Date_____ Name_____

	Breakfast	Lunch	Snacks	Dinner
Monday				
Tuesday				
Wednesday				
Thursday				
Friday				

EXERCISE 4 BREAKING STEREOTYPES

These exercises are designed to break stereotypes that are created around the ritual of food.

- Eat at least one meal during the week with your fingers, or using a palm leaf instead of a plate, or on the hand-made your children designed plates, or using a branch instead of a fork, etc.

- No matter how old your child is, s/he can help you decorate the table, cook, or help you clean after the meal. Allow them to play with this activity. Allow them to bake a cake with you, allow them to cook a breakfast for you, allow them to make a sandwich for you. And if they make a mess, make it a rule not to get upset by it at least as long as the exercise last.

- Change the roles, let the children take care of you during 1 meal. Let them 'mother' you, chose your food, prepare it for you. See what happens...

- Do a competition of your table or plate decoration: who will be the most creative in decorating the plate or the table...

- Create your-own 'eating' ritual with flowers, candles, your meditation or a prayer.

- Whenever you can eat all-together.

Mindful Eating   by Nuit

We are all children that need **nurturing**, **love** and **care**. So give your **inner child** that nurturing and love, give yourself back the **joy of preparing healthy and nutritious meals**, joy of experiencing food without TV, reading, working, rush.

with Delicious RAW VEGAN RECIPES
www.artof4elements.com

TRANSFORMATION TOOLS CONSCIOUS PARENTING

MODULE 2 YOUR HOME

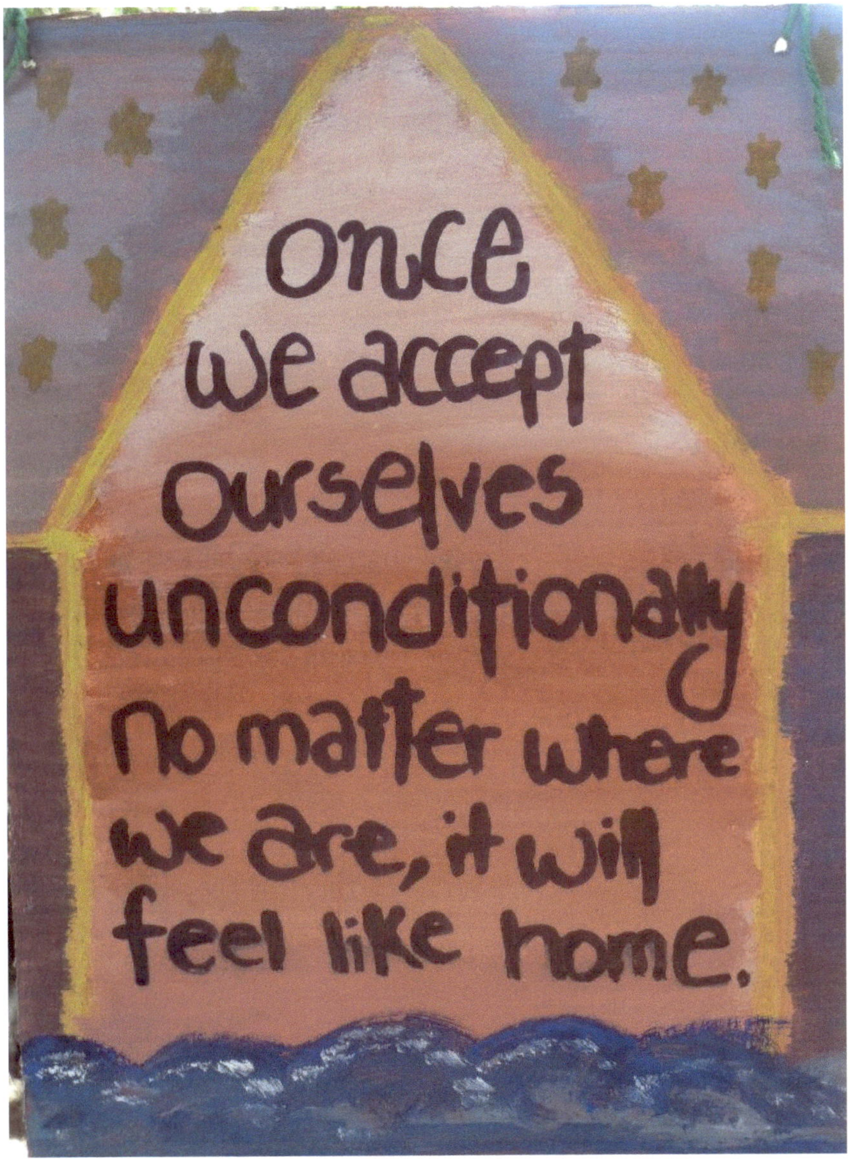

Often the environment we live in mirrors our Soul's state. If we are surrounded by Chaos, our Mind can not function Peacefully. If we love ourselves, we will give our-selves the **gift of Beauty** in everything that surrounds us, the **gift of Harmony** and the **gift of Zen Emptiness**

OBSERVE YOUR ATTITUDE TOWARDS YOUR HOME

YOUR HOME IS A PORT YOU'LL ALWAYS RETURN TO, YOUR HIDING PLACE, YOUR BASE, THE PLACE WHERE YOU TAKE REFUGE, GAIN STRENGTH, LIVE EVERY DAY.

What all of us need is a home with the corner-stone called: LOVE.

Conscious Parenting 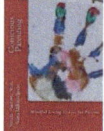 **by Nuit**

'If we wish to have a beautiful, peaceful and safe home, we need healthy expanding roots that go deep into the ground. These roots are our **Routine**, our **Stability**, our **Structure**.'

Everything starts from your home and everything ends there. If we did not develop the basic security that starts at home, we will start feeling insecure within other areas of our lives.

Transform your house into a home full of warmth that is a source of your strength.

The place you live in could become your energy sucker, because you did not pay attention to all the clutter or electrical appliances.

Observe your place.

How many unnecessary things do you have around you?

How many appliances do you have in your kitchen?

How many TVs do you have and how often are they on?

How does your wardrobe look like?

And what about the entrance to your place?

Or your spare room, what kind of clutter do you have there?

If you have a child, how does your child's bedroom look like? Is it appropriate for the age of your child or does it keep unnecessary 'memories' and toys of when your child was younger? How many never opened books do you have, how many never used clothes, how many never used items?

Each item carries an energy and with clutter we get overwhelmed with unnecessary energies all around us. Each item has a color and shape and with clutter our visual surrounding gets disharmonious and we disturb our concentration and attention and concentration and attention of our children.

The amount of time you spend inside your home is an indicator of how comfortable your home is. If you are constantly on the go, outside of your home, this might indicate your subconscious wish to 'escape' from home and its surroundings. Staying at home at all times, might indicate that you are afraid of the contact with other people and surroundings.

There is a subtle balance between outdoor and indoor activity that will naturally occur once we enjoy our home and once we feel love within and outside of the home.

ANSWER THE FOLLOWING PERSONALITY QUESTIONS RELATED TO YOUR HOME & ENVIRONMENT YOU LIVE IN

Observe your environment & write down the major observation you have about home you live in.

My Home

	Your Bedroom	Living Area	Your Kitchen	Your Car	Your Desk	Your Dinning Table
Harmony		Too noisy				
Beauty	Beautiful			Perfect, just new		
Clutter	TV		Too cluttered			Full of documents
Use		TV, computer, games				Working on DT
Missing		Too noisy			No desk	
Beauty				Perfect, just new		

Use your-own words to describe your environment.

CONSCIOUS PARENTING COURSE   MODULE 2 YOUR HOME   OBSERVATION EXERCISE 1

Date_____   Name_____

Observe Your Home	Entrance	Living Area	Yard
Harmony			
Beauty			
Clutter			
Use			

List of sentences that describe your environment:

Observe Your Home	Child's Bedroom	Kitchen	Store Room / Cellar
Harmony			
Beauty			
Clutter			
Use			

Questionnaire 1 Describing Your Environment

Now, write down a list of sentences that describe your environment.

Answer to what extent you feel these statements are true. Rate your statements from 1 (really bad) to 5 (I am super happy with it)

		1-5
1	I designed a home that I love and that inspires me and others who visit it	
2	I surround myself with beauty	
3	My space is not clattered with books, unused boxes, sentimental items, children's toys, newspapers	
4	My car is clean in and out	
5	I live in a peaceful environment	
6		
7		

Write the answers of the Questionnaire

After you have answered your questions, meditate on answers and where the problems within your life might be.

Use a colored marker to highlight areas that might need improvement. Add whatever you feel is missed out from this list. The ranking from 1 to 5 will indicate your list of priorities.

Action Item from the Personality Questionnaire

Study each answer that you are not happy with and determine what precise action you would like to do to change your state of body, mind, emotions.

Write down the areas that need improvement.

Be specific.

CONSCIOUS PARENTING   MODULE 2 HOME   QUESTIONNAIRE 1 DESCRIBE YOUR HOME

Date_____ Name_____

Conscious Parenting

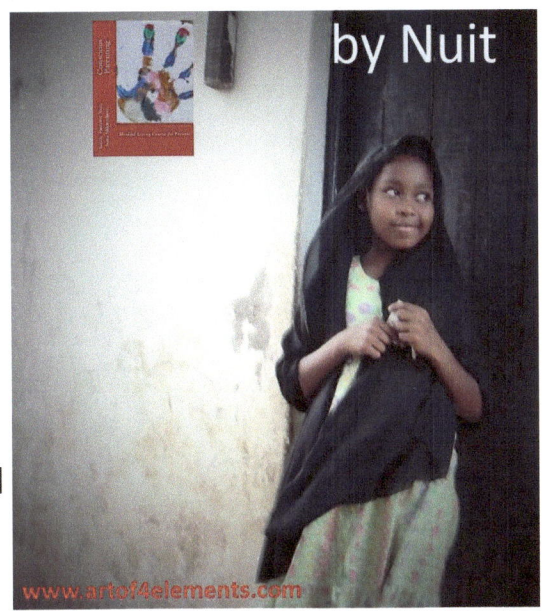

'If we do not respect our **Earth**, the **World of Emotions** & Mental development will suffer. We all need **Rhythm** in our food consumption, sleep patterns, cleanliness & exercise regime. **This Routine does not come naturally** and it is learned and exercised from very young age.'

My List of Priorities:
Items Marked as 1, 2 and 3 are:

My Home Improvements	Time Scale

Exercise 1 Defining Areas of Improvement within Your Home

If your problem is your home, your car and the constant mess that follows you, be specific about it. Write down what exactly the problem is:

My space is constantly cluttered (Example)			
Because of:	**Action Items:**	**What stops you from doing it?**	**Any alternative?**
My wardrobe is full of clothes that I rarely use, my shoes are all over the place	Clear your wardrobe	I hate throwing away clothes!	Find a charity and donate them – they will appreciate it and you will start your recovery
My desks and tables are cluttered with papers, books, electronics	Clear your desks	The mess is beyond me	Mess accumulates, start by tackling a room / a desk at a time.
My pipes are leaking, my refrigerator, or hair-dryer is broken	Fix them or buy a new one	I always forget to do it	Call the plumber now!
My plants are dying	Take care of them	I have no time for plants	Find time – early morning is the best for 'plants time'
The noise level around me is constant and intolerable	Switch off TV, Radio, isolate your flat from outside noise	There is always something interesting ON	Have times during the day when you do not have any noise around you. Practice silence.
My Storage shed is fullof items that I do not use	Empty / Fix / Repair	It is beyond me	Create a 'clear all' day. Fix 1 room at a time. Give presents f.
I have too many appliances on the kitchen counters	Clear, remove, store	I love cooking	Give some to your mum, she will love it!
Papers and games all over the dining room table	Clear, remove, store	Children love to play games	No games at the table!
Unorganized makeup drawers	Clear, remove, store	No time	If not used or opened for centuries – remove
I have too many never to be opened books	Clear	Love Books	Donate to a Church Fare

Now write the action items that you would like to pursue, so that these conditions change. Devote time to creating an ordered and harmonious surroundings, your Soul will love it!

CONSCIOUS PARENTING   MODULE 2 HOME   EXERCISE 1 YOUR HOME IMPROVEMENTS

Date_____   Name_____

Your Home Improvement Area:			
Action Items:	**What stops you from doing it?**	**Any alternative?**	**Done or Not**

Write a date by which you would like to execute your action list.

Let's do it! What you can do today, do not leave for tomorrow!

Action	By Date	Done √

EXERCISE 2: BEAUTIFY YOUR HOME

YOUR HOME AND BEAUTY

Create a place where you can feel comfortable, where you can feel relaxed, where you can feel **AT HOME**.

HOME IS NOT JUST A PLACE, IT IS A STATE OF BEING

Get into a habit of lighting candles, and lighting incense. It is a wonderful habit that connects us to the energy of **Peace**.

Keep your home aired properly. **Cultivate the good quality air**. Do not smoke inside your place, and always have enough fresh air within your spaces.

Avoid air-conditioned spaces, stick to the fresh air.

Many different breathing problems are linked to air-conditioning - asthma, coughing, sneezing, itchy skin, sore nasal passages, frequent colds, frequent headaches, allergic reactions.

If you live in a climate that demands the use of air-conditioning units (40^0+), make sure that you regularly check and clean the filters. The filters get loaded with more and more particles, reducing airflow and they become a source of air pollution itself. Keep in mind that nature has four seasons, and that we have been accustomed to live in the nature for thousands of years. **Use air-conditioned wisely, to help you live within your environment, not to rule your environment**.

Have in mind that the body experiences a certain amount of stress when it is forced to go from a boiling hot environment into a cool air of an air-conditioned room.

Keep the plants out of your bedroom - during the night they breath out carbone dioxite that might disturb your sleep.

To enhance the creativity of your children, and to break some good old stereotypes, chose a wall inside of your place and allow your children to draw on it, to write on it, to do anything they like to it

EXERCISE 3   CONSCIOUS USE OF COLORS

Symbols & Signs ➔ Now Imagine White Light

Colors vibrate, colors are alive... Use colors consciously to support you, not disturb you.

If we wish to support a particular state of being, or a particular activity, we wear or surround ourselves with a particular color.

Physical Body is represented by **RED**

Mental Body is represented by **YELLOW**

Spiritual is the color **BLUE**

USE COLORS CONSCIOUSLY
Learn more about Feng Shui that uses colors in all of its recommendations.

Using color is a great way to create a peaceful feel in your spaces.

In Feng Shui, color is one of the 9 ways that you can influence your life.

Human color experiences are often cultural, however there are some universal guidelines to the way colors influence us.

Red is a physical color. Biologically red can be a signal of danger. It represents **masculine energy**. Its high vibration and strength draws attention to itself. It means energy, action, and excitement. It is often used to express sexual love.

Red, in its softer version becomes Pink, that is associated with **feminine energy**, and within its depths it hides shades of Spiritual Growth.

Blues give a quiet feeling. It creates a meditative atmosphere, relaxing tensions and refreshing the body. It is often used in bedrooms. Blues in combination with reds give violet, a colour associated with Spirit.

Orange is a color of adventure that inspires enthusiasm. It is optimistic and sociable. Orange vitalizes, inspires and encourages creativity.

Yellow is an illuminating and uplifting color. Yellow stimulates mental clarity and analytical processes. It is associated with logical reasoning and it is often used in offices. Yellow could be a warm and happy color. However, too much yellow can cause anxiety, and nervousness.

Green Green is the color of our natural environment, of growth, of plants, of spring… Add green to your spaces, add plants to your surroundings to support your growth.

Exercise 4 Implement Simple Feng Shui Tips for Your Holistic Home

- **The door and entrance** should be tidy and welcoming, *In Feng Shui* your entrance symbolizes opportunities to find you.

- *In Feng Shui,* water represents wealth and money flow. Make sure you keep the toilet seat closed, as well as the bathroom door. This will keep the wealth from flowing away from you!

- *In Feng Shui* you should not store your things under your bed. What is underneath you affects you. Clutter under the bed symbolizes subconscious blocks in your relationships. Also, never work out of your bedroom; it should only be used for rest and relaxation. Take TV, Computers, radio, mobiles out of your bedroom.

Fix what is broken (especially glass)

Throw away what is not used

Make sure that all your drains are functioning properly

Avoid Sharp angles pointing at you

Make sure all your windows are clean

Allow natural light into your spaces

Have healthy and strong plants

Module 3 Conscious & Unconscious Thinking

Our mind is constantly busy with thoughts and feelings about our past, present or future. To stop it from useless constant chat, we must learn how to hear this noise, how to become aware of it, and to transform it through **concentration into mindfulness**.

CONSCIOUS AND UNCONSCIOUS THINKING PROCESS

Taoists with their concept of **Yin** (unconscious) and **Yang** (conscious force), Yogis with **Ida** and **Pingala**, that are two opposite energy forces that flow through our body, Cabbalists with the female and male side of the **Tree of Life**, all guide us towards the examination of both: our conscious mind and our or collective unconscious mind.

Researchers say that conscious mind controls our brain only 5% of the day, whereas the subconscious mind has control of our thoughts 95% of the time. A human being has 70,000 thoughts per day.

Mindful Being by Nuit

'With 70,000 thoughts a day and 95% of our activity controlled by the subconscious mind, no wonder that it feels as though we are asleep most of the time. To awake, we need to train **Self-Remembering** and **Mindfulness**.'

www.artof4elements.com

CONCENTRATION

With 70,000 thoughts a day and 95% of our activity controlled by the subconscious mind, no wonder that it feels as though we are asleep most of the time. To awake, we need to train self-remembering and mindfulness. Since, mind is in a constant movement, since thoughts attack us from everywhere, to quiet it we need to use its movement, to stop the flow of thoughts, we need to find an object of concentration and focus on it with all our might.

Unconscious or **subconscious** is vast like an ocean, and the awareness and wakefulness need to be trained for a long time. For a successful training one needs to have a strong **Will Power**.

It is not natural to wake up at the break of dawn to meditate, and yet it is the most beautiful experience one could have. It is not natural to challenge the existing beliefs, and break the existing patterns, and yet once you manage to do it, you create space for the new patterns to form, the ones that are filled with love, acceptance, knowledge, and you give yourself a chance to spiritually grow.

Your Child's Focus

It is very important that we exercise focus whatever we do at any particular time. It is important that we dedicate all our powers to the action in question, that we 'perfect' our activities, that we do not do things mechanically, but passionately whether we wash the dishes, cook, garden, or clean. Our actions are the best when we concentrate while doing them. Various spiritual groups use divine dedication to achieve this 'happiness in action'. Some Hindu priests would devote the cooking of their meals to their Gods, so that the meal is done perfectly as though the Gods will actually taste it. Stay with the quality of wonder from the beginning to the end of the activity, no matter how many times you have repeated it. This is a conscious exercise and we should do it as often as possible.

Practice focus with love with your children and they will approach every single task with focus and love. The focus is closely related to our course's 2nd principle: **Rhythm**. To be able to exercise 'focus' in day-to-day life, a child should have time to relax, time for silence, and time to perfect activities, to focus and wonder.

Mindful Being   by Nuit

'**Mindfulness** increases the awareness of the **Nature of the Mind**. If we learn to Control our Mind and **Listen to our Souls** we can consciously choose to be **Joyful** instead of sad, **Peaceful** and **Loving**, **Alert** and **Relaxed**.'

www.artof4elements.com

Happiness Test, Conscious Parenting Self Development Course

How Happy Are You?		How Happy Is Your Child / Partner?
1. In general, I am a happy person		1. In general, s/he is a happy person
2. I have bursts of happiness and bursts of unhappiness		2. S/he has bursts of happiness and bursts of unhappiness
3. I am neither happy nor unhappy		3. S/he is neither happy nor unhappy
4. I feel unhappy and depressed most of the time		4. S/he feels unhappy and depressed most of the time

Now, consider your state of happiness and the % of time you feel happy, neutral or unhappy.

This statement best describes me:

1. > 75% happy
2. 50% neutral - 25% happy - 25% unhappy
3. Neutral most of the time
4. > 75% unhappy

If your **Happiness** score is >75% happy and you feel most of the time happy, you are either already working on yourself or you are in love :).

If you are 50% neutral and 25% happy with 25% unhappy, you belong to most of the humanity that is labeled as 'normal'. Whether or not you chose to do this course, have in mind that happiness is a skill that could and should be trained, that love can expand beyond measure, and that living your highest potential IS very exciting and rewarding.

If you are neutral most of the time, it is time to add some flavors to your life - some spiritual strawberries and cream...

If you are > 75% unhappy and mostly feel unhappy and depressed it is the right time to take control over your life and help yourself start moving towards deeper and lasting **happiness**.

Learning **the Art of Self Development** we learn about power of , , , true , and we become aware of the possibility to live life in harmony with ourselves, our neighbors, our relatives, our parents, animals, plants, and the planet Earth. Through a process of **self-discovery**, we will learn **mindfulness**, we will get in touch with **conscious behavior** and **change our attitudes** so that we are not ruled by instincts, habits and someone else beliefs.

QUESTIONNAIRE 1 YOUR THINKING PATTERNS

We will help you examine your Mind and your every-day thoughts. We will look into your conscious and sub-conscious addictions, and we will help you identify your strengths and weaknesses.

This questionnaire contains a number of statements that describe your attitude towards your Mind.

Read each sentence and rate them from 1 (really bad) to 5 (I am super happy with it). Answer to what extent you feel this statement is true for yourself and for your child.

Your Thinking Patterns	1-5
I rarely watch TV	
I do not listen to music constantly	
I am not an Internet addict	
I am not a mobile addict	
I am not games / gambling addict	
I am not a workaholic	
The noise level around me is healthy	
I have an inspiring hobby	
I read inspiring books	
I have good friends and I socialize with inspiring people	
My work inspires me	
I meditate / pray / am in contact with nature regularly	

Your Child's Thinking Patterns	1-5
S/he rarely watch TV	
S/he does not listen to music constantly	
S/he is not an Internet addict	
S/he is not a mobile addict	
S/he is not games / gambling addict	
The noise level around him/her is healthy	
School inspires her/him	
Reads inspiring books	
Has enough time to play	
S/he does arts and music	
Practices sports	
Has friends	

WRITE THE ANSWERS OF THE PERSONALITY QUESTIONNAIRE

After you have answered your questions, meditate on answers and where the problems within your life might be. Use a colored marker to highlight areas that might need improvement. Add whatever you feel is missed out from this list. The ranking from 1 to 5 will indicate your list of priorities.

ACTION ITEM FROM THE PERSONALITY QUESTIONNAIRE

Study each answer that you are not happy with and determine what precise action you would like to do to change your state of body, mind, emotions.

Write down the areas that need improvement. Be specific.

There are a number of mental states that evolve around your Thinking Patterns and that can potentially cause you problems. These are related to negative mental fixations that eventually end up being your emotional problems.

EXERCISE 1: MY WORLD, OUR WORLD

Draw 4 circles with the following titles:

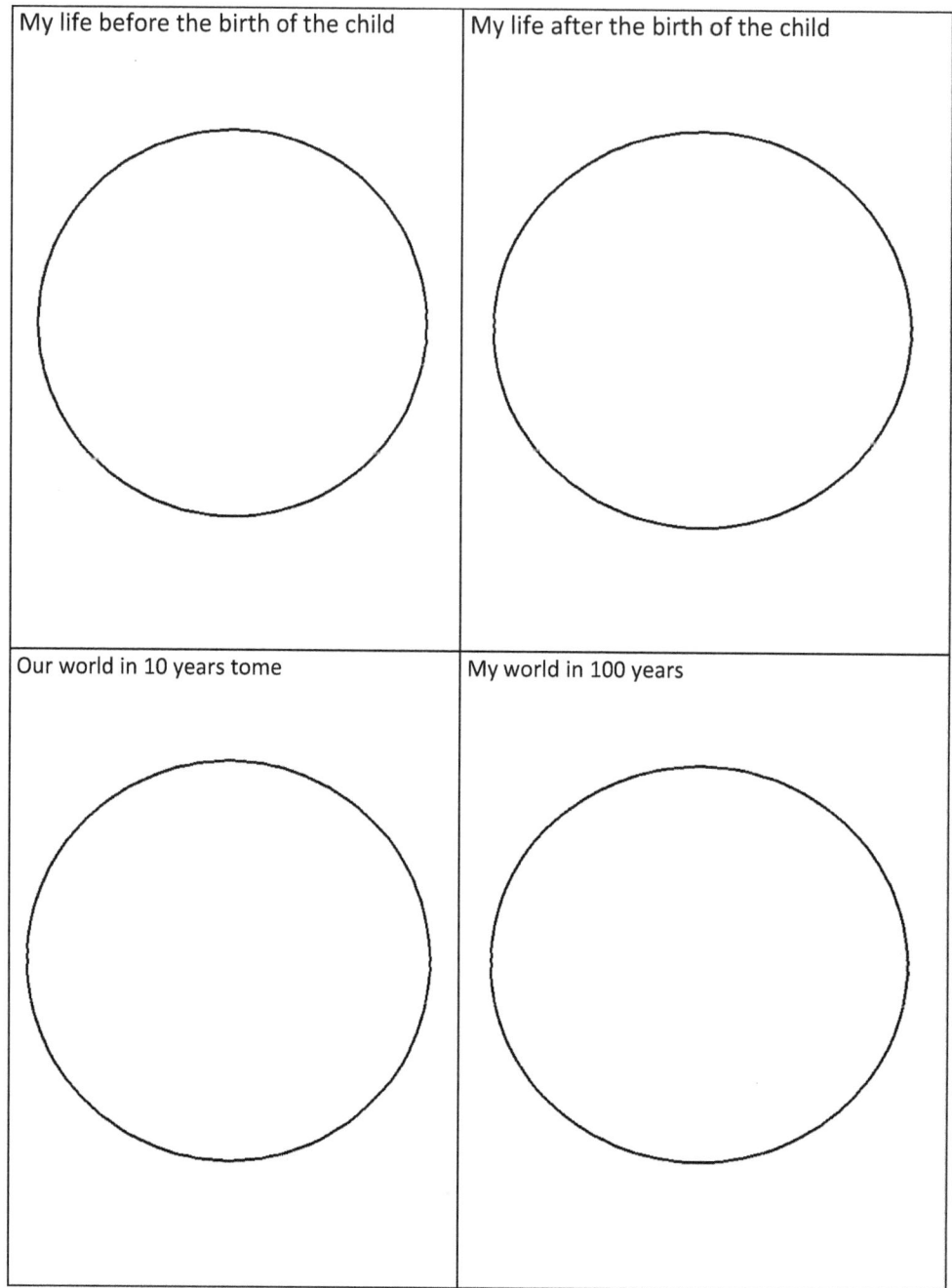

Write within the circles 3 words that describe your emotional state; and 3 activities that inspire you.

Then, give us a sentence of an image that describes your life. For example, if you see yourself within a swimming pool surrounded by children, or as a mum surrounded by house-hold chores, or a taxi driver to your children, write these sentences down.

Be as truthful as you can summarizing your life within this one drawing / sentence.

Meditate about the answers and see what this exercise has given you.

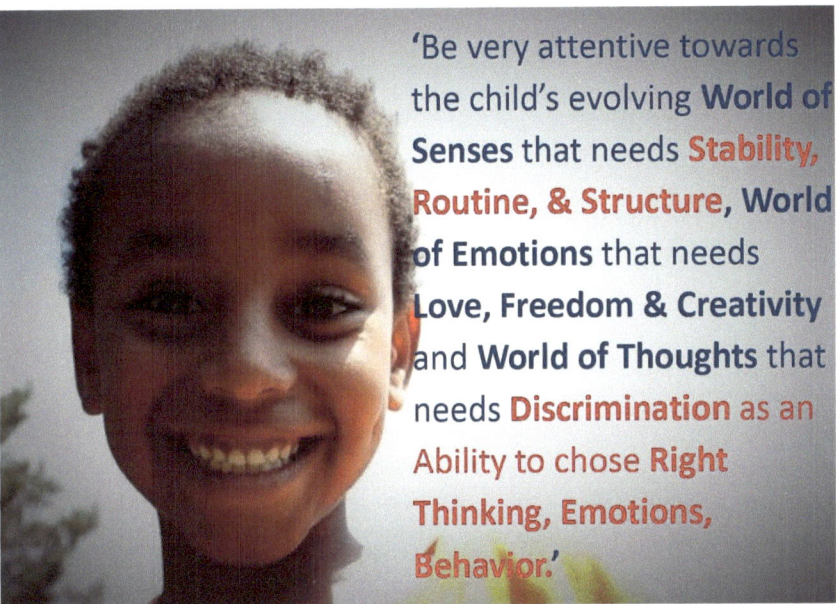

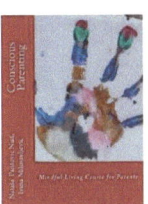

EXERCISE 2 IDENTIFY YOUR MENTAL FIXATIONS

Some of these mental fixations could be described as:

Mental Fixation	Emotional Consequence	Positive Alternative
I did not fully forgiven those who have hurt me, deliberate or not	I do not trust people, do not take risks, do not talk to strangers. Isolation	**I forgive**, I trust, I love
I judge or criticize others constantly. Life is never good enough.	I judge and criticize myself constantly. Cynicism and Bitterness. Anorexia, bulimia	**I will not judge or criticize.** I believe in myself. Self-confidence. Creative Flow
I gossip or talk about others	My time is constantly wasted by useless talk. I am not honest any longer	**I will not gossip.** Words are a creative force. I am careful with my words
Often I do not honestly say what I want and need	I keep everything within, get angry and explode or get sick	**I will practice honesty and truthfulness**
I never admit when I am wrong	I argue constantly, I am not careful with words and deeds	Healthy humor. We all make mistakes
I am jealous or I envy other people's success	I do not help others so others do not help me. Feel quite lonely	I rejoice with others in their success
I constantly compete	I do not work with others in harmony	Working together is **inspiring**
I blame others / circumstances for everything. I am very indecisive.	Everything is against me. I can't start or finish a project. I luck self-confidence. I am not able to make decisions.	I take risks and am able to materialize my wishes. I take **responsibility for my happiness**.

Write your own list

Start with brainstorming, noting down what your mental fixation might be:

- I do not always express my true feelings.
- I am constantly angry at my children
- I am constantly arguing with my partner
- I am quite pessimistic

EXERCISE 2A GENERATION GAP ANALYSIS

Please consider the generation gap, the difference in age between you and your child. Assuming you had your child at 30…

Age	Physical	Mental	Emotional
30-35	At the peak	Strong	Balanced
0-5	Very weak	Not visible	Explosive
Consequence	- No physical exercise - No proper sleep - **Physically exhausted** by work around toddlers - **Healthy Food Habits** are shaken by constant demand for sweets and junk food	**No proper mental exchange** with: - Children - Partner or - Friends	'Balanced' is slowly moved 'Out-of-Balance' with: - 'why is s/he crying again?', - 'what else can I do to help?', - 'what the hell am I doing wrong?' to: 'what the f___ do you want now?'
35-40	Some misbalance, some disease, still strong	**Shaken** by: constantly listening to 'twinkle twinkle little star', watching cartoons & focusing on baby talks, home work, teachers and various demands	**Racked** – shouting constantly, repeating same sentences and the same breakfast, school, sleep routine over and over again…
5-10	Strong, full of energy	School time – exams fever	**Often Frustrated**: luck of time for physical activity, for play, and parents that always shout
Consequence	We stopped walking or We spend hours walking	We stopped talking or We spend hours talking	We stopped hugging or We spend hours playing and cuddling

At the age less than 10 children absorb the world like sponges, they learn sub-consciously

At the age 10+ children are becoming more consciously aware of their parents behavior and they start remembering their parents' acts...

At the age 40+ parents often no longer care how children will remember them...

Age	Physical	Mental	Emotional
40-50	**Body is aging** and diseases and weaknesses start interfering with day to day life	Pessimism increases. All is taken personally. Challenges by children become offensive or This is the **time to share** wisdom, secrets, beauty, and join in the challenges of youth and growth.	**Close / Defensive / Hurt** or **Open / Excepting / Excited** for experimenting is always exciting
10-20	Very Strong, full of energy	Strong, **challenging existing beliefs**, structures	Experimenting

At the age of 20+ children are ready to move out and start their own Life experiment loving, growing, expanding, still waiting for their peak at 30.

At the age of 50+ parents are ready to direct their journey inwards, to stop worrying about their little ones, and to re-learn how to live their lives without them.

Check the above generation gap analysis and highlight with a marker statements that are your truths. Consider each one of them. These will help you highlight the areas that might need improvement within your life.

Exercise 2B I Want More Syndrome

One of the syndromes that is constantly part of our nature is: I want more syndrome. No matter how much do you give to a child you will hear a repeated sentence 'I want more'. If you are not careful with your response, you might experience problems later on:

Negative Response to 'I want more' syndrome	Consequence	Positive Alternative
'I will buy you this or that if you are good', 'St. Claus will give you presents if you deserve it'	I have to be 'good' to please my mum or St. Clause, so I better not say what I want and feel... I do not express my true feelings.	**Children are not good or bad**. They are an expression of **Divine Life Force** and as such we can learn lots from them
'Your friends have it, so you better have it too!'	I have to be the same or better than my friends and the value is determined by 'more expensive', same as in TV add, or magazine. The values get completely disturbed and lead to luck of self-worth.	**Beauty** is inside of us, and every creature is special and has its place within this **Cosmic Play**
Buying more expensive goods at all time	My friends appreciate me because I have money and expensive things. Money and expensive things define me.	**My friends** love me for who I am. I value myself & work to build deep friendships
Buying more and more and more	My bedroom is full of toys I do not play with, but I want them around me at all time. Accumulation Syndrome	**I let go** of my old toys, give them to children who appreciate them. Making other happy makes me happy.

Exercise 2C I WANT TO COMPETE AT ALL TIMES

This is another mental fixation that can become our truth, our way of life, our invisible shadow that stops us and our children from expressing our highest potential.

Negative Response to 'I want to compete' syndrome	Consequence	Positive Alternative
Constant competition at school	I am jealous or I envy other people's success. I do not help others so others do not help me. Feel quite lonely	I rejoice with others in their success
Constant competition with friends or siblings	I do not work with others in harmony. No respect for the winner. No appreciation in seeing somebody else good work.	Learn **healthy competition** playing team sports. **Working together is inspiring**. Admiring the winner is nurturing. learn from them.
I never admit when I am wrong	I argue constantly, I am not careful with words and deeds	Healthy humor. We all make mistakes

What to do if our child has a competitive spirit? Do we kill the spirit?

We need to re-direct our focus from the desire to win our opponents towards the wish to improvement our own potential.

We need to redirect the focus to compete against time, not another person, against our own previous results.

Bring back the child's attention towards the awareness of the experience. Ask your child: 'Did you enjoy the game did you enjoy the experience?' Allow the focus to shift towards the enjoyment, towards the play, towards the desire to be better and master the game.

Exercise 2D Attention Focus Deficit

The rhythm of our lives and our day-to-day habits might cause our children to become depressed, obese, they might end-up in front of computers or TV screens at all times, having behavioral problems, becoming sick, or experiencing attention deficit hyperactivity disorder.

Consider the hyperactive state of mind when you are creating your list of Mental Fixations.

Negative Response to Attention or Focus Deficit	Consequence	Positive Alternative
I will give you a new stimuli at all times, we will be 'doing', 'doing', 'doing'	I can not do an activity longer than 5 minutes. I constantly want to change my surroundings. Happiness is always on the other side	We try to do any activity the best we can. We do not change it after a few minutes to replace it with another stimulus.
We tried all different sports and all different extra curriculum activities, and we can not stick to any of them	I do not work with others in harmony. As soon as there is a conflict I leave. Changing activities constantly, later on in life, lead to not stable work, friendships, not stable love life.	Longer we stay practicing, better we become. We enjoy the art of doing it 'perfect'. We take care of our relationships.
I am focused on your behavior / life at all times	I argue constantly, I create problems so that my mum or dad will 'react'. Otherwise the life is boring. This lead to an attitude, later in life, that problems are the only way to feel the life force flowing	I let you explore and be on-your-own. We grow through learning. Life is a wonder full of mystery. Learning from flowers, stones, we are never bored.

Understanding our conscious and sub-conscious patterns, and the ways of thinking will help us learn about ourselves and develop patterns that are empowering, so that you can express and experience your highest potential. Write the main challenges that stop you from perfecting your body, mind and that create 'noise' when you listen to your soul

Children are a beautiful caricature of our own states of mind, observing them, and their patterns we come closer to our own sub-conscious gibberish.

START WITH SMALL STEPS: REDUCE THE 'MENTAL NOISE' AROUND YOU (SWITCH OFF TV AT BREAKFAST), IMPROVE YOUR SLEEP, WALK TO THE GROSSER, MEDITATE WHEN PUTTING YOUR BABY TO SLEEP…

Some tips if your child is hyper…

- Forgetfulness, losing things, speedy finish of tasks, starting tasks before we say the instruction, making unnecessary mistakes, fidgeting at all times, all indicate that a parent needs to work to improve the focus of the child, and his or her concentration.

- If the child is in a constant movement and is not able to sit down, it is likely that the child's rhythm is disturbed by too much: TV, computers, games. Children that are on the 'move', at all times have the word 'action' written a;; over them. They do not understand the meaning of 'sit-down' meals, a peaceful moment that has no radio, no external stimuli, no TV, no structured extra-curriculum activities, no rush, no aimless walks, no aimless chat, no free aimless play.

- If your child is restless at all times, and you give him all the physical support necessary (safe and warm home), and you also respect the rhythm and routine, it might be that the child wants to tell you something about your relationship with your partner. The restlessness of your kids could be a reflection of the emotional war that might be going on within the house. This war might be of a silent type but the kids will feel the tension even if you and your partner are extremely 'polite' to each other. Be very careful about this emotional and mental set-up because it can become very disturbing and damaging for the child;

- Try to finish the tasks that you start with your child;

- Give a reason for the task that you give to your child, with the reason and a concrete purpose, the child will find it easier to finalize it. 'We are doing this for the Granma', 'we are preparing for the celebration', etc.

- Praise your child immediately when the child does something 'special'. There are many occasions for the praise. Sarcasm and negative comments are dangerous because they hurt our little ones.

- Whatever you say to your child say it clearly and consciously. The use of words is very important especially if you have a child that has a problem with concentration.

Conscious Parenting by Nuit

'**Every child** is an individual with a different growth rate & a varied and vast potential. Respecting the talent that is hidden within each child, **we respect their potential to become Kings of their Trade, or Saviors of the World to come.**'

www.artof4elements.com

- The golden words are 'SLOW DOWN' and 'EASY'. The golden surrounding is: 'QUIET'. Noisy outside activities should be avoided. Crowded surroundings should be avoided.

- Long as silent as possible walks, with no music or other surrounding 'activities',

- Avoid unnecessary changes and unplanned events as much as possible.

- Planning as a skill needs to be trained within the focus deficit kids. They move their focus very quickly from one item to the next. Try to treat your environment consciously. Remove all the visual or audio stimuli and clutter, leaving only the items for the tasks that you are performing at the moment. Visual and audio clutter will constantly defer the attention of your child.

- Always talk to your children after a fight you had. Come back to a space of peaceful communication and love that is necessary for the trust between you and your little ones.

- Create a warm and safe home. Use priorities, rhythm and structure to guide you through your life. Home should be an oasis of peace, your warm nest, and your secure hub.

- Give your child a daily responsibility for a plant or an animal, daily feeding, walking, and watering. All of the above help build a sense of responsibility.

- Sit with your children when they do their homework or when they eat. It is important that they feel your presence and support to sit down.

- Sport is good for all children. Too competitive sports could be too tiring for the children with the focus deficit because they tend to be extra competitive. Practicing contact sports might also be difficult, because they could be too aggressive for the children that get too excited easily. Practicing a sport like volleyball or table tennis enhances one's ability to play with others and yet have no disadvantages of many 'contact' sports.

- The whole family needs to support all of the above training.

- Suggest to your child to write a diary. Support this activity and allow your child to express through writing. Do not read your child's diary. If you would not read your partner's diary or anybody else's diary, respect your child, and do not read the diary. This child's connection to the daily diary might become the only 'escape' route, the only way the soul can express itself within the daily hassle and bustle. Try to introduce this wonderful tool within your kids' lives. It might save you lots of trouble later on in life.

CONSCIOUS PARENTING MODULE 3 THINKING EXERCISE 2 IDENTIFY MENTAL FIXATIONS

Date_____ Name_____

Mental Fixation	Emotional Consequence	Positive Alternative

EXERCISE 3: BE MINDFUL

This the week when we start practicing MINDFULNESS

We eat, walk or talk but we are not aware of our-selves. If we are aware of ourselves, we are awake.

The essence of the **Self-Remembering technique** is that while we are doing anything – reading, singing, talking, tasting – we must be aware of the Self who is reading, singing, talking or tasting. The awareness, the energy, the life is that Self that is present within us.

In **self-remembering** there will be **no thought** whatever we are doing.

Walking next to the sea: the sounds are there, the wind is there, we are there with the sun, with the breeze, and with our breath and awareness of our body moving, but without our thoughts.

When eating, when bathing suddenly remember yourself, and stay as long as you can – **remembering**. Only effort is needed: a **continuous conscious** effort. Whenever you remember to do it, remember yourself. Repeated efforts to **self-remember** lead to higher states of **consciousness** and an **awakened** state of being

EXERCISE 4 TRAIN YOUR WILL POWER

WILL POWER OUR WILL-POWER NEEDS TRAINING

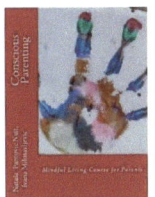

www.artof4elements.com

Willpower needs to be trained every single day, so that it could be later used in the process of **Spiritual Development**.

You train your **Willpower** when you challenge your existing structures, when you go against your instincts, against the hunger, when you go against your sleep, when you challenge your limits whatever they are.

Write your-own list of actions for exercising Willpower during the duration of this Course. These are some of our suggestions:

- do not eat immediately when you are hungry – wait a couple of minutes, challenging your hunger
- do not sleep immediately when you are sleepy – wait a couple of minutes, challenging your sleep
- at the end of your shower, use cold water, challenging your comfort zones
- swim in cold waters
- wake up early to walk or jog
- wake up early to meditate
- run marathon
- climb Mont-Everest
- fast on water for more than 24 hours
- stay without Internet for some time
- stay without TV and Radio for some time
- do not have an orgasm after 11 minutes of sex with your partner but enter into the magic of making love that might last hours
- do not get angry, even though circumstances are against you

Willpower is the basis of all Self Development Work

Train your Willpower

With the strong Willpower you will be able to invite the lady Love into your life and let Her rule from the centre of your Heart.

Be careful to guard your child's willpower.

Respect IT, respect the child and his opinions and wishes.

Remember, every time you hit your child, you kill a bit of his or her willpower.

Too dominant mother, too protected children, grow into people who luck in decisiveness.

At all times, give your children more freedom to decide what they want, need, and wish to do.

Let the child make his own decisions. Let the child ask questions. Free child thinks with his own head.

Consciously Practice avoiding the word NO

There is always an alternative way to say NO. Practice it!

Chose a day when you will not use the world NO.

Work on the acceptance!

One of the ideas is to destruct the child with something else. If a child is small, tickle him. Or just allow a little bit of what s/he wants, children get satisfied easily.

Mindful Being   by Nuit

'Learning the **Art of Self Development** we learn about power of **Mind, Consciousness, Mindfulness, True Love**, we become aware of the possibility to **Live Life in Harmony** with ourselves, neighbors, relatives, parents, animals, plants, and the planet Earth.'

www.artof4elements.com

Exercise 5: Practice Concentration and Focus

Exercise 5A Follow my Rhythm

Rhythm is an amazing tool for concentration. Children love rhythm. Once you wish your child to learn something, you can use rhythm as a tool to help your child concentrate, focus, repeat, learn. Rhythm also good as an exercise that changes focus of the child. If the child is disturbed, or it has a problem with concentration and attention deficit, you can use simple rhythms to practice with the child the attention span.

Start with a simple rhythm, exercising around 3 minutes, clap your hands repeating a simple beat. Ask the child to copy you. You will clap for around 5-6 beats and the child will copy these beats. Make your exercises more complex and longer as you go along. As long as the child is following you, you can increase the time and complexity of the game. During the exercise, keep the structure fixed, bringing the child back into the 'following' mood. At the end of the exercise, when you are satisfied with the results, allow the child to improvise as much as s/he likes and at one point you will together start creating music.

You can do this exercise as long as you wish and as long the child feels entertained.

Motto of the exercise is: keep the rhythm, follow me, calm down and focus.

This is a good exercise for grown-ups too, you can use it when you are depleted of energy or 'fed up' of whatever is happening around you. It is constructive and it diverts your attention into a game….

The more complicated version of this exercise is done standing up on one leg, changing legs and with different hand movements. Clapping will stay constant, but you will change the leg, the position of your hands, or you will turn while clapping, and the child should mirror your movements together with mirroring the beat. You can do this exercise with drums and with percussion instruments. If you do not have an instrument, you can use simple sticks and drum your beat with the sticks.

EXERCISE 5B LET'S JUMP TOGETHER

We sit for far too long. We study sitting down. We sit in the cars, we sit in the classrooms, we sit at home in front of the TV. No wonder, our kids after all that sitting can not concentrate and hold the book and 'sit' and read. Once your child is too tired of 'sitting' and gets up to walk, becomes restless or nervous, you can do together this simple and effective exercise.

Stand up and jump and ask the child to follow you. Jump with the rhythm following the beat. Jump on one leg, jump on both legs, jump from leg to leg, create your own variation of the game. This is a great work-out for both yourself and your child. After the first round, ask the child to create his or her own movements, and you will follow him.

This exercise is done to improve the rhythm and the focus of the child, to instantly change the mood, to 'shake off' the tiredness, and it is great if a child needs to sit for longer time inside studying.

Conscious Parenting

Through the Process of **Self-Discovery**, we learn **Mindfulness**. Getting in touch with **Conscious Behavior** we **change our attitudes** so that we are not ruled by instincts, habits & someone else beliefs.

www.artof4elements.com

by **Nuit**

Exercise 5C Beading

There is magic in beading. Creating beaded jewelry doesn't only make of you or your child jewelry designers but also helps you improve a variety of different skills. Beading is a magic dance of beads, your **imagination**, and **concentration**. You can use beading to help yourself and your child relax and meditate.

This is also an excellent play activity, promoting children's' development within:

Fine Motor Skills
Various sizes of beads promote different grasps. Many components of making a beaded jewelry increase coordination in fingers.

Visual Memory
A child needs to remember the beading pattern and use it all along its creation.

Eye-Hand coordination
Threading beads onto a string involves coordination of the child's hands, eyes and it requires concentration.

Creativity and Planning
Creating a necklace helps children work with a range of skills: decision making process, pattern and materials choice, creation of own beads from scratch.

Group Work
In a group, beading promotes sharing and cooperation, as children need to share beads.

Beading will also provide a sense of accomplishment in completing a project
It offers freedom of self expression and encourages creativity. A child can see an artwork that is created by him or her from its very beginnings

Overall, it is FUN and HAS many benefits!

For children with difficulty using their hands and fingers, try using larger beads with larger holes. For children with visual problems, use large, brightly colored beads. Use this activity for children with Attention Deficit Hyperactivity Disorder. It will help them learn to focus for longer and longer periods of time. To increase the difficulty of the task you can use smaller beads so that the children can concentrate better.

Exercise 5D Hands on a Shoulder

This exercise is used when a child is disturbed, when it yells, throws objects or it is focusing on something else, when you feel that your words do not manage to 'access' into the child's brain. Put your hand gently onto the child's shoulder, change his or her focus. In this way you will:

- bring the child into this present moment
- bring yourself into this present moment
- you respond peacefully on stressful situations
- you train your anger

With this exercise, all of us stop for a moment to let the anger pass, because within the anger we will not manage to do anything. We should try to achieve the mental state where we listen to each other, understand each other. With the motion of kneeling down we say, now I am your height, I listen to you, take it easy, relax, calm down, I am here with you, I listen to you, you are safe and I love you and I want to help you.

This exercise can be used when your child is scared.

When the child is screaming, just have in mind that within NLP (neuro linguistic programming) it is researched that the best way to communicate with somebody who is emotionally disturbed is to use his or her tone of voice, rhythm and paste of breathing and movement, reducing the tone one scale, and scale by scale slowly leading the child to a peaceful voice, movement, and breathing. You just can not calm down somebody who is screaming with a voice that is completely low. For him or her to hear you, you have to use louder voice and lead him down to a peaceful voice gradually.

EXERCISE 6: DRAW YOUR MANDALA

'The "squaring of the circle" is one of the many archetypal motifs which form the basic patterns of our dreams and fantasies... Indeed, it could even be called the archetype of wholeness'... The mandala really is: 'Formation, Transformation, Eternal Mind's eternal recreation'. from Mandalas, C. G. Jung.

According to **Jung**, **mandala** is a **magic circle**, the symbol of the Self, formed by **archetypal forces** of the unconscious that the artist is not aware of during the creation of the work. The **symbols** and images come from the collective unconscious, these are **primordial images**, which reside in each one of us.

Draw a circle, let the shapes and colors come from the depths of your **Soul**. **Express yourself.** Play with colours, play with shades.

Start drawing from the centre. Do not limit your imagination. Do not compete. Just draw. This is your circle. This is your **mandala**. Let it represent you.

Draw a Mandala end Remember to Enjoy the process, Remember to Play, and Love Your Work of Art!

Exercise 7: Transform Your Anger

Practice Separating from your Anger

In the moment when you are angry, when the flow of the anger energy is within your body, shaking every single cell, focus on your body, focus on your hands, focus on your breathing.

Consciously come out of your body and observe the anger, the way it activates all your sensory organs, the way it interacts with your skin, with your brain, with other feelings and thoughts.

If you are not able to focus on anything else but anger, get out of the room and walk quickly just observing your breath. **The breath should be deep and prolonged**. Then, after around 20min of fast walking, separate from anger, become an observer, there is the **Self** that observes your body and the anger.

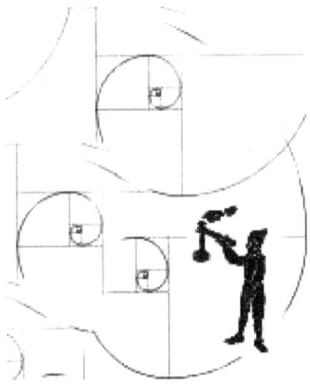

If you are unable to go for a walk, count till 20 and back. Repeat if necessary.

Put your hand on your stomach.

If your child is angry put your hand on its shoulder. Both actions are designed with the intention to calm-down. To slow-down. Say to your anger: easy, easy. Say to your child: EASY… Easy…

> *'Anybody can become angry - that is easy, but to be angry with the right person and to the right degree and at the right time and for the right purpose, and in the right way - that is not within everybody's power and is not easy.'* **Aristotel**

If you are angry with your child, become aware of this emotional energy of anger: what does it do to you, how do you react, how do you follow it, at which point you can stop it?

Can you move this point to an earlier time? Can you not follow an angry thought, word, action and feel sorry afterwards?

Can you ignore the negative reaction and come back to a more rational one?

Once you have acted in anger and you feel sorry about it, tell your-self about it, tell your child about it, do not feel guilty but act differently next time.

Ask yourself: Why did I act angrily? What to do with that energy?

Sometimes we feel anger because we feel we are losing control, some other times we feel helpless to change the situation around us. Some people are at all-time angry because they live lives they do not like.

Say what you feel and why, instead of diving deeper into anger. Admit your mistakes and say sorry. If a child is angry change its focus onto a different activity.

Try conscious swearing, it is an interesting tool that allows your 'anger' to burst without physical violence.

Transform Your Thoughts Attacks

We all know of times when we can not concentrate and when our attention goes into 'unwanted' direction. Reading a page of a book six times, unable to 'see' it, is a good example of this 'disorder'. During these times we are visited with many **'unwanted thoughts'** and **concentration** becomes difficult.

We all experience **obsessive thinking**, when we are jealous or have just finished a relationship or fallen in love. Our ability to **concentrate** and be **mindful** is also disturbed by all the technological devices that we have: mobiles, e-mails, TV.

The quality of any life experience is within the **change of focus**. To experience anything fully we need **mindfulness**, we need to learn the art and magic of **concentrate**.

If you have one of your 'thoughts attacks':

- go for a walk,
- go for a swim or
- go for a jog

The **physical activity** is the best for the 'obsessive thinkers'. If you an emotion 'attacks' you, you are angry with somebody, first go for a walk, jog or a swim and then try to transform this emotion into a positive one.

Put on the music and start dancing. Dance for at least 20minitues. Jump, scream, dance any way you like. When you finish dancing, sit for a moment and observe your body, and your breathing.

Sing! Singing is **healing**

Conscious Parenting   by Nuit

'A child is a **Soul**, a **Unit Consciousness** materialized on **Earth** to learn, fulfill its purpose contributing within the **Matrix of Gaia**. Our parents fought for 'Expression of Thoughts', 'Equality', we now have a task to fight for the **Supremacy of Love over Control** within all **Areas of Life**.'

www.artof4elements.com

Task 1 Start with your Daily Meditation

Silence is healing. Silence is creative. Silence is necessary. **Regular meditation** is a way to clear your mind from clutter of thoughts, a way to train **concentration** and to focus on specific themes.

Concentration

Our **Mind** is constantly active. Seeking **stillness** within the Mind that is in motion is impossible if you do not use the motion itself. When the surface of a lake is still, we will be able to see, experience, intuitively sense the ocean of our sub-conscious and to tap into the magic of super-conscious. This is impossible when the surface is agitated by waves of our thoughts, emotions, habits, fears.

In order to still our mind we will learn how to understand the body and the influence it has on our mind. The art of meditation is the art of stillness, the art of motion within no-motion, action within no-action, visualization and concentration.

Chose an object of **Beauty** that inspires you and use it as your object of **meditation** – a rose, a tree, a crystal, light…

Concentrating our mind on light, love, peace, or pure consciousness, we allow the mind to keep 'busy' while we connect with the source of power, love, peace and knowledge using powerful imagery of **positive imagination.**

Create your own **meditation**, and follow it!

Human Brain and its Magic

Mindful Being by Nuit

'A **thought weaves into another thought**, seeking the other.
The thought world has its-own **Inner Life**.
A rose acts upon us through its **symbolism**, through its **beauty**, through our **conscious** & **sub-conscious mind**.
Meditating we tap into the **thought form of 'rose adoration'**.

www.artof4elements.com

'I MUST BE WILLING TO GIVE UP WHAT I AM, IN ORDER TO BECOME WHAT I WILL BE.' ALBERT EINSTEIN

A HUMAN BRAIN IS TRULY EXTRAORDINARY

A healthy brain has some 200 billion neurons. Conscious mind controls our brain only 5% of the day, whereas the subconscious mind has control of our thoughts 95% of the time. A human being has 70,000 thoughts per day. The brain requires up to 20% of the body's energy despite being only 2% of the human body by weight.

LIVING OUR HIGHEST POTENTIAL

Somewhere, within our brain, **we have a potential** for higher mathematics, complex physics, art, and amazing richness of thoughts, feelings, and sensations. Somewhere, within our brain, **we have a potential** to understand the magic of Divine Creativity. However, we are mostly controlled by our brains, and we are yet to learn how to best use its potential.

Perhaps this is the task of **the next phase of our evolution** - utilizing our brains better, understanding the 95% of its sub-conscious functionality, becoming more creative, less bombarded by useless thoughts, more focused, and more peaceful.

Jill Bolte Taylor, PfD,, a 'human brain' scientist, who recovered from a massive left hemisphere blood clot in her book 'My Stroke of Insight' talks about her experiences during the eight years that took her to completely recover. She was unable to walk, talk, read, write or recall her life. However, she refers to this state of her being as Nirvana, a word used to describe a profound peace of mind.

RIGHT AND LEFT BRAIN

Describing the right brain, she says that the right brain is like a parallel processor. It thinks in pictures, it is non-verbal, it is non-linear, and creative. The right brain has no sense of time, it is playful, it sees humor, and it is lost in the flow. The right side of the 'human brain' is compassionate and it is associated with the heart. It is intuitive and takes us into the peacefulness of the world around us.

The left brain is like a serial processor and it is interested in the past and future. It thinks in language, and is concerned with the details. It is logical and it is the critical analytical part of our being.

The traditional educational methods, its curriculum, and the exam focus, ensure that we emphasize the development of the 'left brain' hemisphere, and with this approach the students quickly lose motivation and the interest for the science and its magic. Two fundamental assumptions of formal education are that students retain knowledge they acquired in schools, and that they can apply them in situations outside the classroom. But is this correct? How much do we really remember and how relevant our knowledge is? The likes of Albert Einstein, Leonardo da Vinci, and Mozart created their master pieces from a place of inspiration, and creativity. It is likely that they had a capability to fully utilise the virtues of both brain hemispheres.

Mindful Being   by Nuit

It was during the **Renaissance** that creativity was first seen, not as a matter of **divine inspiration**, but as a gift of a great learned man to imitate **God's ability to create**. As **Prometheus** stole the fire of the **Gods** and brought it to the mankind, humanity needed to steal the secret of **'creation'** from Gods and understand its **essence**.

To understand children's capability to learn, educational psychology develops and applies theories of human development.

Rudolf Steiner's model of children's development links physical, emotional, mental and moral development. In his approach he equally values rational and imaginative approach to learning, his schools teach art and dancing not only as a way of expression, but as a way of understanding and mastering cognitive thinking. An example of an alternative method of learning is a movement therapy included in the Waldorf curriculum called: Eurythmy. The word stems from Greek roots meaning **beautiful** or **harmonious rhythm. The dance is used** to awaken and strengthen the children's expression and to stimulate imagination.

Eurythmy works with mathematical forms, beginning with a straight line and curve, and proceeding to more complex geometric figures developing a child's coordination and concentration. Rods or balls are also used in exercises to develop precision in movement. Philosophically, it acknowledges a child's capacity to communicate through non-verbal gestures. **Eurythmy** is made up of discreet movements that represent various phonetic sounds. The feelings & thoughts have gestures that are beyond our conscious awareness. **Eurithmy** attempts to explore the variety of feelings & thoughts through the form, movement, language, rhythm, color and form. Through this art children learn the wisdom of emotional intelligence that helps their holistic growth.

> Walt Streightiff *'There are no seven wonders of the world in the eyes of a child. There are seven million.'*

PRACTICE DIVERGENT THINKING

Mindful Being by Nuit

Somewhere, within our brain, **we have a potential** for **higher mathematics**, **complex physics**, art, & amazing richness of **thoughts, feelings & sensations** Somewhere within our brain **we have a potential** to understand the **Magic** of **Creative Thinking**

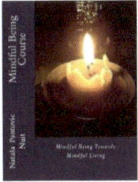

Divergent thinking is essential for creativity and for what is creativity. It is the ability to see lots of possible ways to interpret a question and lots of possible answers to it.

It is a thought process used to generate creative ideas by exploring many possibilities. Instead of taking obvious steps and walking along a straight line, one looks at different aspects of the situation, creating different results.

Divergent thinking is often used as a parallel of convergent thinking that follows a particular set of logical steps to arrive at one solution. All standardised tests stipulate this type of thinking.

In their book and Beth Jarman describe a longitudinal study they conducted on 1,600 kindergarden children aged three to five. They gave them eight tests on divergent thinking and an astonishing 98 per cent of the children scored within the creative genius category.

Five years later, they re-tested the same children, now aged eight to 10 and only 32 per cent scored in the creative genius category. Five years later only 10 per cent of the children scored in this category. In tests of over 200,000 adults over 25, only two per cent scored enough to be classified as creative geniuses.

Divergent thinking tests measure an individual's ability to generate multiple approaches to solving a problem. The tests typically use simple questions such as: what are the uses for a flower pot?

An average person would have 10 to 15 answers to this question. A genius of divergent thinking would come up with a hundred possible answers, and they do this by changing the concepts of already existing thinking – can the flower pot be 10 metres wide, or can it be made of rubber, and so forth.

So what really happens with the universal **mental capability to think divergently**? What happened to those 160,000 children during their school years?

Classic Schools Educational Models and Creativity

The classic school model encourages students to adopt fixed mental models of how things work, discouraging creative thinking and problem solving. Mastering other people's mental models seems to kill an individual's ability to think divergently and wonder creatively.

We are all born with this capacity to think creatively but during the years of schooling, this capability deteriorates drastically.

Confucius: 'I hear and I forget. I see and I remember. I do and I understand.'

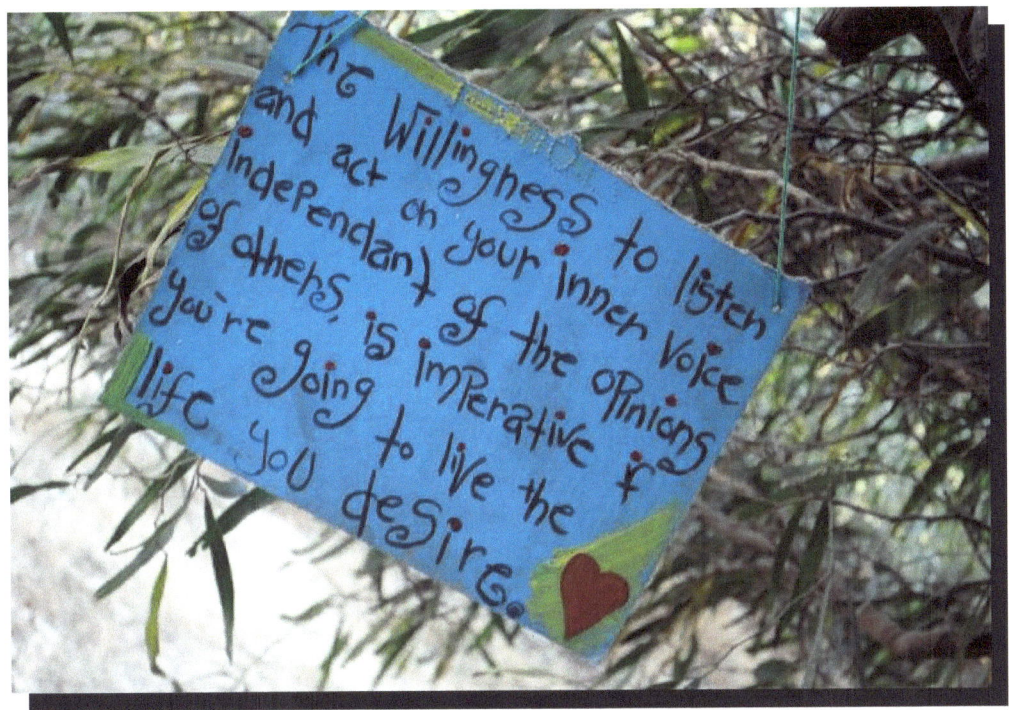

BRAIN AND THE ENVIRONMENT OF LEARNING

The brain is a highly complex organ. The neocortex is the largest portion of the human brain. The majority of complex thought occurs in this part of the brain. Research proves that the neocortex does not function properly when people are under stress or afraid.

The classroom environment has to be safe place for students to experiment, make mistakes and take risks. The environment has to be safe to fail, revise and try again.

RIGHT BRAIN LEFT BRAIN

The brain also has two distinct hemispheres, left brain versus right brain. According to the theory of left-brain or right-brain dominance, a person who is 'left-brained' is said to be more logical, and analytical, while a person who is 'right-brained' is more intuitive, thoughtful and creative.

To fully develop both hemispheres of the brain, it is important to vary thought processes so that children use both convergent and divergent thinking, both the linear, and the creative thought processes.

Divergent thinking is mostly found among people who are curious, willing to take risks, and persistent. Research shows that musicians are more likely to use both hemispheres of their brain and more likely to use divergent thinking in their thought processes.

Promoting Divergent Thinking

Activities which promote divergent thinking include:

• Encourage your child to learn how to ask questions;

• Learn how to think and be silent – allow your children to think and explore using their-own learning techniques, allow them to invent new ones, give them time and space for reflection;

• Create bridges to abstract concepts using common experiences, experiments. You should not separate learning from life; they need to find ways to use nature as a learning setting;

• Let your children write their-own stories. You can tell stories to each other, or create a story together. Allow your imagination to flow. Create your-own stage sets where you can act out scenes from books or stories that you have created.

• Work as a group: Change roles, mother should take a role of a child, father of a mother, child of a father, etc. This game can teach you many things about your child and about yourself;

• Use creative writing – writing anything that comes to mind about the given subject;

• Utilize both music and art: Draw only with colors, do not include the shape within your work, allow the colors to merge and create its-own wonder. Also, draw with your hands, the effects are amazing;

• Practice sport – working with tactics, movements and techniques, and teamwork;

- Create rich, stimulating environments using materials created by student. Changing displays regularly to provide a stimulating environment for brain development.

> **Einstein** *'I never teach my pupils, I only attempt to provide the conditions in which they can learn.'*

PRACTICE CREATIVITY

CHALLENGING BELIEFS

Creativity refers to the invention of any new thing that has value. Someone creative has the ability to learn from traditional ideas and create new ones.

To be creative we have to choose to be different from everyone else. Learning the **skill of creativity** is about learning to challenge the existing, learning to trust one's idea, and working hard to change the world that is by default stuck in the space of 'conventional'. Creativity is an essential ingredient of one's spiritual development.

CREATIVITY AND CHALLENGING EXISTING BELIEFS

Challenging the beliefs about the world we live in and the machinery that makes it work is an essential step within the **creative process**. At all points of origination of a product, solution, or an artwork, we have a choice to reject our invention and go back to the 'norm'. At all points of the process of 'creation' we are challenged by the 'norm' and we can deny our-own mind-set, energy and feelings. Learning to access the necessary creativity within our being and learning how to get inspired from the world around us is an essential ingredient of the creative flow.

Each of our ideas starts in the mind and it is manifested in the outside world if we have the capability to do so, or if we manage to 'sell' our invention to the people who can materialise them for us. So learning the skill of creativity, is about learning to challenge the existing, learning to trust one's idea, and working hard to change the world that is by default stuck in the space of 'conventional'.

Creativity as Divine Inspiration or Human Trait

It took some time for the humanity to accept 'creativity' as a possible human 'trait'. It was during the Renaissance that creativity was first seen, not as a matter of divine inspiration, but as a gift of a great learned man to imitate God's ability to create. As Prometheus stole the fire of the Gods and brought it to the mankind, humanity needed to steal the secret of 'creation' from Gods and understand its essence.

Moving from imitating and copying, to innovating and using our talents wherever we are can take time. First we need to master the particular skill: musicians have to know the rhythm, architects should know engineering concepts, artists must learn about colours and shades, writers must have the knowledge of grammar. Then we need to open our minds to the possibility of being different accepting our uniqueness.

Innovation & Creativity

When we use our imagination to develop a new idea, the idea is inevitably structured in a predictable way, following already existing concepts. Our schools train us to think as convergent thinkers, aiming for a single, correct solution to a problem, whereas creativity demands divergent thinkers who generate multiple answers to a problem because the aim is to mediate inspiration from the unknown, to create something new.

> Dalai Lama *'Share your knowledge it is a way to achieve immortality.'*

Incubation may aid **creative problem-solving**, because it enables 'forgetting' of existing clues. We are constantly bombarded by 'solutions' so creative minds need to stay isolated from the formulas given by society, seeking for the answers in most unpredictable places

CREATIVITY - OPENING TO NEW POSSIBILITIES

A mind should not be thought to passively observe the world, but instead constantly test hypotheses to actively manipulate the environment. The expansion of mind happens when we are open to the new possibilities, when we learn how to be inspired by nature and music and by most versatile forms of art.

Our **Emotional Intelligence**, the **expansion of our mind-set**, our **capability to interact with the world** are all closely linked to understanding this magic of the '**divine inspiration**' of creativity.

> *'You're never too old, too wacky, too wild, to pick up a book and read to a child.'*
> **Dr. Seuss**

MODULE 4 TIME / LIFE WASTERS

Often we do **waste time unconsciously** and we need to apply a conscious effort to record this time and activities, so that we become aware of the wasters of our life. Awareness is half of the answer. Once you are aware of where does your time go, you will do something to change this pattern.

QUESTIONNAIRE 1 YOUR TIME WASTERS

We highly recommend that you spent 4 days observing the amount of your free time you spent on Social Networking, Games, watching Tv, on the Net or your Mobile Phone. After the observation period rate each item from 1 (really bad) to 5 (I am super happy with it). Answer to what extent you feel this statement is true.

Where does your time go?

- Wasting time watching TV
- Wasting time on Social Networking
- Wasting time on mobile / Internet
- Wasting time with games
- Wasting time gossiping, talking about others
- Wasting time sleeping
- Wasting time in laziness
- Wasting time in useless thoughts / fears / worries
- Too much of my interaction with friends / family / loved ones is shallow
- I am constantly surrounded by noise – of TV, Radio, Work Environment, etc.

WRITE THE ANSWERS OF THE PERSONALITY QUESTIONNAIRE
After you have answered your questions, meditate on answers and where the problems within your life might be.

Use a colored marker to highlight areas that might need improvement. Add whatever you feel is missed out from this list. The ranking from 1 to 5 will indicate your list of priorities.

ACTION ITEM FROM THE PERSONALITY QUESTIONNAIRE
Study each answer that you are not happy with and determine what precise action you would like to do to change your state of body, mind, emotions.

Write down the areas that need improvement.

Be specific

CONSCIOUS PARENTING   MODULE 4 TIME WASTERS   OBSERVATION EXERCISE 1

Date_____ Name_____

Your Time Wasters	Day 1	Day 2	Day 3	Day 4
TV				
Games				
Social Networking Sites (Facebook, etc)				
Computer				
Mobile				
Messaging				
eMail				

1 unit = 1 hour of time spent

Your Notes:

_____
_____
_____
_____
_____
_____

EXERCISE 1: MASTER YOUR DAILY HABITS

Emails, ads, text messages, phone calls, and chatting keep us **BUSY** but they overload our minds and over-complicate our schedules. No wonder we're stressed and out of balance! A typical American receives and processes over 197 messages - emails, ads, text messages, phone calls every day.

SWITCH OFF YOUR MOBILE DURING THIS WEEKEND!

- Yes, it is possible to live without a mobile during the weekend, try the old way of phoning people, it is quite interesting

SWITCH OFF YOUR COMPUTER DURING THIS WEEKEND

SWITCH OFF YOUR TV / RADIO DURING THIS WEEKEND

DO NOT READ ANYTHING DURING THIS WEEKEND

TAKE OFF YOUR WRIST-WATCH

DO NOT USE YOUR CAR DURING THIS WEEKEND

Spend time with your loved ones not in a hotel, traveling, or busy with different sets of impulses.

Stay just with yourself, without any technology, and observe the power of Synchronicity that exist within our lives, that we can experience when we are not overloaded with 197 messages sent from friends and strangers of all sort. The Universe will reward your experiment, will reward you for taking risks and you will be training your sense of inner perception.

A Few Ideas to keep your life inspired while you switched off all the technology:

- Meditate
- Play an instrument (re-discover your guitar or just start playing jembe)
- Play with your kids or your sister's kids, Play with your pets
- If you are a dad – cook with your kids; if you are a mum – go and play football with them
- Dance
- Talk to strangers
- Walk, exercise, spend time in Nature, Laugh

Human Brain and Technology

Inspired or Lost within Technology Matrix

We live surrounded by an increasingly complex matrix of impulses allowing strangers of all sorts (TV, media, Internet) interfere in our mental, emotional and spiritual development. Understanding this intricate network and how does the human brain interacts with it is becoming our door to happiness and health.

The self or the personality is a bundle of socially influenced traits that emerges and gets formed gradually. We are shaped by our parents and neighbors, by our religion, the media, by various marketing agendas of major corporations, by our state's politics, by the way we behave or misbehave towards our-own body, our mind, environment, animals and plants, and our planet Earth. So, what would we need to do to understand the importance of a healthy body, to manage our emotions and nurture love for our friends and family, to become aware of how we can make a positive impact on our society or the environment, or discover the purpose of life and ways to be happy?

Human Brain and TV

A great deal is known about our behavior and TV, and our emotions and computer games, because there have been thousands of studies on these subjects. The researchers have all asked the same question - whether there is a link between exposure to violence (on TV or within a game) and violent behavior. Most of the studies answered: 'yes – the link is there'. According to the AAP (American Academy of Pediatrics), 'Extensive research evidence indicates that media violence can contribute to aggressive behaviour, desensitization to violence, nightmares, and fear of being harmed.' An average American child will see 200,000 violent acts and 16,000 murders on TV by age 18...

None of us wants to see our children or our loved ones depressed, obese, in front of computers or TV screens at all times, having behavioral problems, being sick, or experiencing attention deficit hyperactivity disorder. However, the rhythm of our lives and our day-to-day habits might have an adverse effect on our mental health.

Human Brain and Mobiles

Human brain does some very sophisticated ordering of its incoming nerve impulses. Any information that we are exposed to becomes knowledge when it is translated and related to the personal experience, to the feelings, or desires. When we look at an image, our perception of an image is colored by our emotions. There is a reciprocal relationship between the area of the brain responsible for logical thinking and the area that is the seat of our emotion. Within the world of technology, numbers, letters, adverts, '**human brain**' has to constantly perform little miracles of de-coding, detachment, de-stress, and de-tox to keep us sane and free of diseases. As we grow older, and stronger in our wish to stay healthy and happy, our need for creativity grows, we constantly luck time to be physically active, to read and reflect, to play, and amongst all, we luck the quality time with our friends and family. The interaction with the NET, with the TV, with the computer has replaced the interaction with nature that in its magic way nurtures our cognitive, emotional, physical and psychological well-being.

A group of friends socializing will have a number of mobiles handy on the table, easily within reach for checking e-mails, showing off photos, or answering a call. This invisible 'best friend' and inseparable 'commodity' could prove to be our 'worst enemy'…

A recent study by Andrew Przybylski and Netta Weinstein of the University of Essex observed couples of strangers discussing a meaningful topic for 10 minutes with or without a cell phone nearby. The pairs who tried to 'connect' in the presence of a cell phone repeatedly reported **lower relationship quality** and less closeness with the assigned 'chatting' partner. The studies suggest that because of the many 'entertainment' options phones give us they distort our ability to connect with the people right next to us.

"The presence of a mobile phone may orient individuals to thinking of other people and events outside their immediate social context. In doing so, they divert attention away from a presently occurring interpersonal experience to focus on a multitude of other concerns and interests." said the lead researcher Andrew Przybylski.

A study for the Journal of Behavioural Addictions in the US analysed the data from 191 business students from two universities and revealed that students send on average 110 texts a day, or approximately 3,200 messages a month and check their phones 60 times in a typical day. Nomophobia is the term for people who experience anxiety when they have no access to their mobiles.

Human Brain and Inspiration

An electronic 'connection' interferes with our human relationships. Saying 'I love you' and texting 'I love you' could have completely different connotations based on body language. Discounting the value of nonverbal cues leads to an amazing amount of mis-understandings.

Text messages are used in our romantic and sexual correspondence. A wonderful romantic love letter became obscure. Texting is quick, easy, and convenient and notwithstanding its 160 characters limitation, some people use it to exchange important information with their romantic partner. Messages are often misinterpreted, often edited, forwarded, or written by somebody else. The stress caused by the response expectation is unique for this type of communication. A lack of response to a text message from a potential romantic partner is often deciphered as a form of rejection.

So, how to help our minds stay inspired and enthusiastic and our relationships stay healthy?

- Limit your time with TV, mobiles and computers;

- If you are spending the time with people you really care about, you might want to re-consider the habit of reaching for your phone to reply to a text message or checking your e-mail.

- Spend quality time with your loved ones, re-invent your time together: sing, dance, do art together, or explore learning a new language;

- **Experiment, challenge the existent, and stay curious;**

- Stay in constant contact with nature.

Mindful Being   by Nuit

How to Avoid Negative Impact of Technology?

- Stay in constant contact with **Nature**
- **Limit your time with TV, mobiles & computers**
- Spend **quality & creative time** with your loved ones: **re-invent** your time together: **sing**, **dance**, or explore learning a **new language**.

Exercise 2: De-clutter and Simplify

Toys and physical and mental clutter

Today's life style has given us an opportunity to buy lots of toys for our children, at any age, at all time of the year. Gone are the days when we used to play with one doll for years. What type of the effect this way of life has on our children's brains, and what type of crazy consumerism attitude are we creating within our children from an early age? Why we should be careful with the clutter that we are creating in our children's lives from early on?

If you 'suffocate' your child with different toys, you are not allowing him or her to learn through exploring, to deepen its focus, to analyze, research, create objects of play, you hinder its creativity. The child has no longer time to play with the toys, becomes a friend with the toy, love the toy and has an intimate relationship with it. The toys are nowadays changed constantly and this creates confusion in their tiny brains. The child with the room full of toys is no longer able to focus, because of simple visual clutter. Whatever is in hands will not be enough, if the other toy is also reachable.

The toys are made to be perfect, so they do not allow for the expansion of imagination. Different alternative schools such as Montessori and Waldorf suggest that early toys should be hand-made and without specific features, ie. a doll without a face, a ball made of cloth, etc, so that children's imagination can work its wonder. Perfect toys do the job instead of children, stopping them from the exploration game.

If you have a child, you will know the truth of 'never to be used toys'. You wonder, how can that be that your child does not play with toys but constantly asks for the new ones. Remove the clutter from your child's bedroom, remove the toys and stop buying them. Let the children create their-own toys, let the world of nature becomes the source of toys.

Also, children love the world of grown-ups. Real cooking utensils are extremely interesting as toys, photo cameras, music instruments, gardening, taking care of animals, playing chess board games, the world of grown-ups can beautifully be a part of their world without any extra clutter.

TRANSFORMATION TOOLS CONSCIOUS PARENTING

MODULE 5 FEELINGS

Free Your Conscious & Sub-Conscious Mind

We will help you examine your world of feelings and emotions.

OBSERVE YOUR FEELINGS

We are capable of such an amazing range of Feelings. Feelings make us Human. The Emotional Intelligence is a skill and an art form. Do you understand your feelings? Do you let your feelings inspire you or rule and ruin your life? Do you connect to your-own Feelings? Are the Feelings yours or do they belong to the rest of the Humankind? Out of the shadow of a Human Soul, out of Conscious and Unconscious Behavior. They can be tamed yet not controlled, they can become our obsession or our Creative Force.

Meditate upon the following words and answer to what extent do you feel this way right now.

- Inspired
- Creative
- Curious
- Loving
- Excited
- Strong
- Enthusiastic
- Full of energy & action

CONSCIOUS PARENTING   MODULE 5 FEELINGS   QUESTIONNAIRE 1 TODAY I FEEL

Date_____   Name_____

Describe Your Feeling	Day 1	Day 2	Day 3	Day 4
Inspired				
Creative				
Curious and full of wonder				
Full of Love				
Excited				
Mentally Strong				
Enthusiastic				
Full of energy & action				

Your Notes:

_____
_____
_____
_____
_____

WRITE THE ANSWERS OF THE PERSONALITY QUESTIONNAIRE

After you have answered your questions, meditate on answers and where the problems within your life might be.

Use a colored marker to highlight areas that might need improvement. Add whatever you feel is missed out from this list. The ranking from 1 to 5 will indicate your list of priorities.

ACTION ITEM FROM THE PERSONALITY QUESTIONNAIRE

Study each answer that you are not happy with and determine what precise action you would like to do to change your state of body, mind, emotions.

Write down the areas that need improvement.

Be specific...

For example:

Once you identified your problems, use the words – I feel:

- Confused
- Lonely
- Guilty
- Distressed
- Stressed-out
- Scared
- Irritable
- Lazy
- Nervous
- Skeptic

Now when you have identified your problems, turn them into your strengths, create a concrete action plan that can help you with your feelings.

Have a virtue per month that you are exercising:

- exercise openness, exercise truthfulness, exercise courage.

EXERCISE 1: EXERCISE AWARENESS

The quality of life is in proportion of our **capacity to get delighted**.

The capacity for delight is within our capacity to pay attention to things around us. So, during this week pay attention to birds singing, to clouds formations, to flowers that greet you, to kids laughing, to a beautiful person that has just passed by.

Be aware of interconnection of all living beings and be alert for the presence of **Divine in All**.

Art of 4 Elements by Nuit

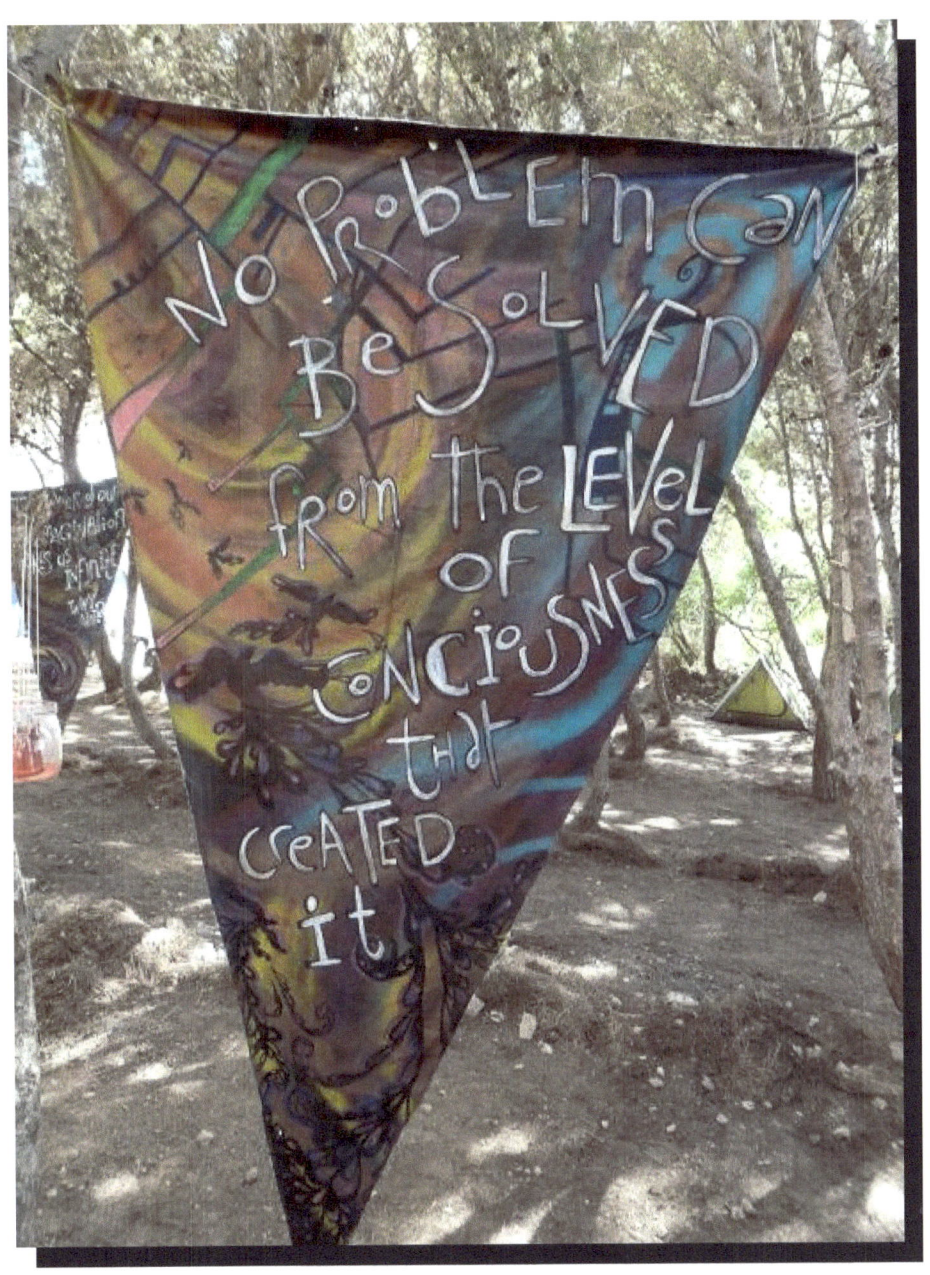

EXERCISE 2: YOUR SOUL'S DIARY

Your Soul's Diary or **Stream of consciousness writing** is done early in the morning, and it is about recording your thoughts, feelings, your day-dreaming. The writing is done without judgment, without conclusions, without any particular intention.

You should just follow your **stream of consciousness**. Do not interfere – write!

This writing becomes the **Diary of your Soul**.

You will find revealing patterns in your thoughts and feelings and you will start exploring the depth of your Soul's secrets.

Writing the **Diary of your Soul** is healing.

Your writings should not be organized into any sort of topics. You should allow yourself to write nonsense, to write rubbish, to write gibberish.

If you get stuck start with recalling your dreams that night and let your **Soul** do the rest of the talking. Try not to read your Diary just after you have written it. Allow it to sit for a week, without any review, or judgment. This will encourage your **Soul** to go deeper into **Truthfulness** and your writings will become more inspired.

Follow the flow of whatever comes along and do it every morning!

NOBODY EXCEPT YOU WILL READ YOUR DIALOG WITH YOUR SOUL

Exercise 3: Practice Virtues

For a week at a time, cultivate a single **noble quality**: love, honesty, clarity, tolerance, non-violence, or positive thinking. **Read about this quality**, **meditate** on this quality, **do art works related to this quality**, talk to people about it, work with it, let IT becomes you.

If you are **practicing virtues** – you will observe your actions in thoughts, words and deeds.

Thoughts are very potent. Do not ignore them. If you think negative of somebody, that thought will poison you and you will turn it against yourself, soon you will be thinking negative thoughts about yourself. That's the law of nature.

But, most of all: **Practice Truthfulness**

Mindful Being   by Nuit

Being **Mindful of our Feelings** we will get **Delighted**. The Quality of Life is in proportion of our **Capacity to Get Delighted** and this is within our **Capacity to Pay Attention**. Be aware of **Synchronicity** among All and Alert to the presence of **Divine in All**.

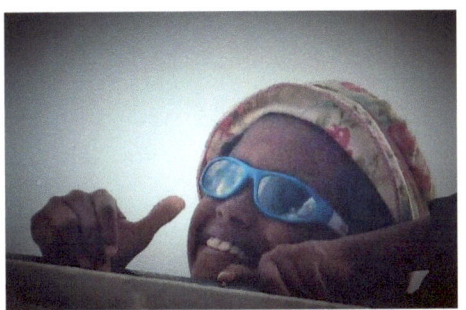

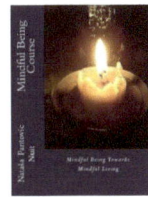

www.artof4elements.com

EXERCISE 3A: PRACTICE TRUTHFULNESS

Be truthful. With the truth you will get other virtues. Don't tell lies. The lies stick onto you, they become a habit and the mind starts uttering them before you are aware of consequence of lying.

Our society is based around little lies that are served to children from very early on. We lie about Santa Claus, we lie about tooth fairies, we lie about little 'do's and 'don't-s, 'can' or can not-s because lying seems easier. However our little ones quickly find out what is the truth and are quick to adopt lying as a norm within their lives. It is easier in long term to practice truthfulness and to have the truth instead of a lie as a normal behavior.

'A child has a deep longing to discover that the **World is based on Truth**. Respect that longing. In our attempt to help children **grow into Inspired Adults**, we wish them to carry the **Youthfulness of their Souls**, and the **Wonders of Childhood into their old age**.'   **Conscious Parenting** by Nuit

WHAT DOES IT MEAN – PRACTICE VIRTUE?

Exercise 3B: Practice Compassion

Practice Compassion

Find an example of the best follower of this virtue.

For example, **Dalai Lama is embodiment of Compassion**.

If you are practicing **Compassion**, read his work about **Compassion**, introduce **Compassion** in your every-days life, put a photo of Dalai Lama on your desk, so that it reminds you about his work and the quality of **Compassion**.

Write about **Compassion**. Watch films that inspire **Compassion**

Meditate about Compassion. **Feel the Compassion** within your heart.

Wake up with a Compassionate thought. Go to sleep with **Compassion** within your heart.

Talk to people about **Compassion.**

Live Compassion!   **Practice Compassion**!

TRANSFORMATION TOOLS CONSCIOUS PARENTING

MODULE 6 CORE BELIEFS

Your Highest Potential is Waiting

Your enemy within are your core negative beliefs. Negative beliefs hide from the consciousness and they get exposed by the magic of mindfulness and awareness.
Mindfulness and Awareness is half of the battle won.

UNDERSTANDING CORE BELIEFS

Core beliefs are at the very essence of how we **perceive ourselves**, and the world around us. Core beliefs are rigid, hard and inflexible. Core beliefs are sentences and words that are repeated so many times that they became our truth.

Core beliefs identify who we are, what we are allowed to do or be, and how do we behave and react to people, experiences and life.

Mindful Being   by Nuit

Our enemy within are our Core Negative Beliefs.
Negative beliefs hide from the Consciousness and they get exposed by the
Magic of **Mindfulness and Awareness**.
Explore Your **Core Beliefs, Challenge Existing,** Train **Mindfulness**, Understand **Beauty**, Work with Emptiness, **Meditate**

Everywhere we turn, someone will tell us how to think, how to look, what to feel, what to say, how to live. The news will give us a message of a dangerous world, the magazines will shape our sense of beauty, TV will teach us that money is happiness and beauty is in the youth, and our consumer society will shape our needs and wants. We are constantly bombarded by the messages of what to believe in, how to think, or what to do.

Children absorb the **beliefs like sponges** from their parents, friends, and teachers, but also from TV, Internet, and the world of media. A child could start believing that s/he is stupid, boring, lazy, non-lovable or selfish. These **core beliefs** become entrenched in our **subconscious**.

Our core beliefs are at the root of our unhappiness, our low self-esteem, our destiny.

If we change our beliefs, we can hope to change our reality

There is a core belief that boys should wear blue, not cry, not play with dolls, and that the girls should wear pink, avoid football, cars and planes and stay in love with stereotypes of Barbie dolls. Stay aware of stereotypes because they form our beliefs and if your little girl does not have a long blond hair and thin body, she might feel rejected if she was bread within this world that adores Barbie dolls and princesses.

Ask your child what is its favourite colour and also ask questions about it. If the answer is pink, introduce the child to different shades of pink, creatively play with the concept of pink, allow the stereotypical 'pink' to grow into your personal 'pink' that might later change into any colour of the spectrum.

Children are like sponges and whatever you give them as a belief, they will easily adopt. If you wish to give your child a possibility of an open mind, when you hear a stereotypical statement, tell the child: 'In some other countries, people do 'this' differently', 'in some other age, people used to do it differently', etc.

The major stereotype that was built all through the ages is that Princes and Princesses can do anything, while the ordinary folks should listen to instructions. This stereotype was supported by numerous fairytales that glorify Princes and Princesses and take a little notice of other people's lives. This can leave an imprint within the mind that says: I am not worth it, I am not equal to the Prince, I should be rich to be noticed, I should have a palace and a horse, and find my happiness within my prince or princesses, I am not as beautiful, etc.

When you are reading books to your children, think about what is the message that you are passing, think about the content of the story that was written during the time of famine, wars, or various catastrophes. Do you really want your children to listen to these messages?

When you read a story, stay with it for a moment. Allow the story and its setting to become alive within your story telling. Do not just jump from one story to the next. Stay with one for a period of time, allow its content, its message, its flow to stay with you and your children. Discuss it during the day, or return to it the next day. If you wish you could also narrate the same story written by the different author, or create your own version of the story.

It is important that we challenge our beliefs and that we develop alternative, balanced beliefs.

Mandela *'Education is the most powerful weapon which you can use to change the world.'*

'Be very attentive towards the child's evolving **World of Senses** that needs **Stability Routine & Structure**. **World of Emotions** that needs **Love, Freedom & Creativity** and **World of Thoughts** that needs **Discrimination** as an Ability to chose **Right Thinking, Emotions, Behavior.**'   **Conscious Parenting** by Nuit

QUESTIONNAIRE 1 MY CORE BELIEFS

This questionnaire contains a number of statements that describe core beliefs, and they will help you identify Beliefs that Guide Your Life.

Read each item and rate them from 1 (lowest) to 5 (highest). Answer to what extent you feel this way right now, that is, at the present moment.

Successful	Unsuccessful
Responsible	Irresponsible
Open	Closed
Happy	Unhappy
Loved	Not Loved
Honest	Dishonest
Relaxed	Tense
Consistent	Inconsistent
Hard working	Lazy
Entertaining	Boring
Determined	Undetermined
Courageous	Fearful

WRITE THE ANSWERS OF THE PERSONALITY QUESTIONNAIRE

CONSCIOUS PARENTING   MODULE 6 CORE BELIEFS   QUESTIONNAIRE 1

Date_____   Name_____

My Core Belief	1	2	3

After you have answered your questions, **meditate** on answers and where the problems within your life might be.

Free Your Conscious & Sub-conscious Mind

Free Mind
Journey to Happiness
Creative Flow
Divine Inspiration

Alchemy of Love

Mindfulness Training

Use a colored marker to highlight areas that might need improvement. Add whatever you feel is missed out from this list. The ranking from 1 to 5 will indicate your list of priorities.

Each member of the family does the questionnaire on his own. Each member of the family can share the answers with the others. This can give you some interesting insight into Core Beliefs of your children, or your partner.

ACTION ITEM FROM THE PERSONALITY QUESTIONNAIRE
Analyze your list of priorities.

Listen to your internal dialogue for:

- 'I can't...', 'I'm afraid...', 'I am not well equipped' 'Circumstances are not just right – maybe not just now'

Become conscious of thoughts that slow down your inspiration, your creativity, your spiritual progress. Focusing on negative qualities is letting fear and habits ruin your chances for happier and healthier life. Diagnose your malady and find its proper cure.

Identify limiting belief   Identify more useful belief

Apart from the virtues that we have already mentioned, the positive beliefs that you can work with are.

- CRITICAL THINKING and ANALYTICAL REASONING
- OPEN-MINDEDNESS and FLEXIBILITY
- LOVE for people around you
- LOVE for plants and animals
- LOVE of learning
- TOLERANCE for DIFFERENT PERSPECTIVES
- PERSEVERANCE and PERSISTENCE,
- TRUTHFULNESS and HONESTY
- ENTHUSIASM and OPTIMISM
- KINDNESS and GENEROSITY
- SELF-LESS SERVICE or MODESTY and HUMILITY
- SELF-CONTROL and SELF-RESTRICTION
- GRATITUDE and THANKFULNESS
- PLAYFULNESS and HUMOR

You can easily find the positive intention of any negative belief – write your own!

Exercise 1 What are your LIMITING BELIEFS

Your Core Beliefs will manifest in life as an inability to do some concrete things like:

Limiting Belief	Positive Alternative
I take ages to make decisions and it is often hard to act decisively. Always change my mind with children.	I will take time to evaluate different options but I will stick to my decisions.
I am a creative person that is stuck in a box of routine and boredom	I will create a set of circumstances that inspire me and keep me mentally and emotionally satisfied
I try my best to control everything around me. I hate failures.	I do not consider a failure as good or bad. I learn from it and I continue entering the challenges, doing the best I can.
I am too busy with mundane to love.	I am never busy to love. I will invent occasions throughout the day and put love into 1st place
My mistakes worry me and discourage me.	I learn from my mistakes. I am grateful to what I have
I believe that we all need to struggle and suffer to grow.	I meditate, read inspiring books, meet inspiring people
I do not like my job or the repetitive nature of my job.	I will change my job. I understand the magic of prioritizing: starting the new.
Worry and pettiness deplete me from energy and give me an emotional fatigue.	I refuse to let worry and pettiness into my life. There is so much beauty around me so I will not waste my time!
I am just not able to do anything, I feel completely drained and depleted of energy.	Life inspires me. I feel confident that as my knowledge increases, all my new ideas usually succeed.

Now, write down what are the Beliefs you would like to adopt. Change the list of your Negative Core Beliefs into a list of Positive Intentions **You are who you believe you are. Your reality is shaped by these major beliefs.** Add the part with negative beliefs that are transformed into positive beliefs.

CONSCIOUS PARENTING   MODULE 6 CORE BELIEF EXERCISE 1 IDENTIFY CORE BELIEFS

Date_____   Name_____

Limiting Belief	Emotional Consequence	Positive Alternative

Exercise 2 Draw a Flower of Beliefs

Draw a flower with 4 petals. In the centre is 'I'. Write down your qualities or virtues that inspire you most.

1st petal

Write people that inspire you and their qualities.   Write a name of a philosopher, scientist, saint that inspire you for whatever reason. Write one word next to each name.

2nd petal

Write skills that you wish to have and activities that might inspire you (music, art, and writing, sport)

3rd petal

Write 2 personal goals for this year that you wish to fulfill. It is recommended that these goals are related to the skills and qualities you wish to develop.

4th petal

Write down something that you have achieved in your life and that makes you very proud. Do not forget to feel grateful for the successes that you already had within your life. Appreciate them and give them time and space in your life.

Purified replacing Matter by Spirit
Cell by cell...
Nourished by **Earth**
Veiled by **Fire**
Carried by **Air**
Dissolved by **Water**
Filled with **God**
Intoxicated with God
Becoming Divine
Metal transformed into **Gold**
Through the supreme Magic of the mastery of
Thoughts and feelings
Evoking the **Infinite Wisdom** buried inside
Impeccably and non-compromising
Living the Infinite Love

Art of 4 Elements
by Nuit

Exercise 3 My Name

Each one of the family members should write down his or her name vertically on a piece of paper and list a number of qualities that have the same first letter as letters of the name.

Draw what this quality means to you…

What is its color, shape, what is the person or animal that represents it?

This can become a little game where you all discuss the qualities and when were these qualities most visible within your relationship.

A   Attractive

N   Nice

A   Aware

An Alphabet drawing used in Steiner Schools

EXERCISE 4 CHALLENGE EXISTING BELIEFS

One of the strongest **existing beliefs** we all have is that we will be happy if other people like us. For other people to like us we try our best to be 'liked' complying with the current 'norm' whatever the 'norm' is. This leads to a major flow of **EXPECTATIONS and DISHONESTY** about ones True feelings and thoughts.

The society has set a norm of **Beauty as a Value**. Youth is Beautiful. To comply with this 'norm' we undertake plastic surgeries, we diet to exhaustion, we develop bulimia or anorexia, but nothing truly helps because at one point or another we DO GET OLD.

To be truthful to ones feelings, you need to distinguish which of the feelings / thoughts are actually yours and which are the product of mass marketing and socially established norms.

My girl tells me that her favorite color is PINK. Do I believe her? Or is it so, because a crazy media machine of our time pushes PINK as girls' color.

If your child tells you that someone is ugly, ask him/her to explain what exactly is ugly, what the ugliness is, tell him that you do not quite understand and leave the child with the question.

My mum, fairy-tales, and society tell me that the **happiness** is within the institution of Marriage. No wonder all hell breaks loose when we discover that we are married and not as yet happy.

Who am I?

What am I?

What makes me happy?

What are the whispers of my Soul?

How to listen to them?

To be able to answer these questions, first and foremost we need to challenge our relationship with the 'norm'.

Chose any of the following exercises to 'break' the chains of society that are tightly woven around your neck:

- Go walking backwards
- Stop next to the street music player and start dancing and singing with him
- Go to a nudist beach
- If you are a man – put on nail-polish on one of your fingers
- Do not wear under-pants
- Stop to talk with strangers
- If in a crowded street, just stop and observe the crowd moving next to you
- If in an argument, choose a point of view that is not yours and argue it as though it is yours
- If you never go by train, try going by a train; if you never go by bus, go by bus
- Invent your-own exercise that challenge your relationship with the 'norm'

Have lots of FUN!

Tasks:

- T1 Meditate in the morning – learn to get in touch with silence within yourself

- T2 Set your clock ½ hour earlier and write a page of stream-of-consciousness writing. From today, do it every day for the next 6 weeks

- T3 Read your Soul's Diary. Reading the words that you have written will give you a shift in perspective and you might be able to identify some of your core beliefs. Reading what you wrote, and observing the words you speak are practices of self awareness.

Transformation tools Conscious Parenting

Module 7 Relationships

This module is designed to help you examine your relationships, your ability to love and tune into your-own and other people's wants and needs.

QUESTIONNAIRE 1 RELATIONSHIP QUESTIONNAIRE

Mark each statement from 1(strongly disagree) to 5 (fully agree) by indicating how much you agree or disagree with it.

- I am in tune with my wants and needs
- I love my-Self
- I feel love and compassion for my parents and I often tell them that I love them
- I get along well with my siblings – we share, we laugh, we play together
- I get along well with my co-workers and manager/staff.
- I have a circle of friends/family who love and appreciate me for who I am
- I listen to my friends when they are upset
- My partner empowers me, he believes in me, and supports what I do.
- I usually discuss my problems and concerns with my friends / partner.
- I spend enough time with friends in good quality exchange

Train Unconditional Love ➡ Conscious Relationships

Conscious Parenting   Module 7 Relationships   Questionnaire 1
Date_____   Name_____

My Relationships	
I am in tune with my wants and needs and I love my-Self	1-5
I feel love and compassion for my parents and I often tell them that I love them	
I get along well with my siblings – we share, we laugh, we play together	
I get along well with my co-workers and manager/staff.	
I have a circle of friends/family who love and appreciate me for who I am	
My partner empowers me, he believes in me, and supports what I do.	
I spend enough time with friends in good quality exchange	

My List of Priorities:
Items Marked as 1, 2 and 3 are:

My Relationships	1	2	3

Write answers to the Personality Questionnaire

After you have answered your questions, meditate on answers and where the problems within your life might be.

Use a colored marker to highlight areas that might need improvement. Add whatever you feel is missed out from this list. The ranking from 1 to 5 will indicate your list of priorities.

ACTION ITEM FROM THE PERSONALITY QUESTIONNAIRE
Study each answer that you are not happy with and determine what precise action you would like to do to change your state of body, mind, emotions.

Write down the areas that need improvement. Be specific...

- My partner makes me doubt myself.
- I find that my partner don't want to get as close as I would like.
- I prefer not to show my friends how I feel deep down.
- It's easy for me to be affectionate and loving.
- I Run after other people in the quest for affection
- I have lack of friends
- My relationship with my parents destroy my self-confidence and I feel a lack of appreciation
- I am not able to attract the type of people I want into my life
- I try to impress others
- I don't have enough time off to socialize / improve my relationships
- I get too easily irritated with my parents
- I get too easily irritated with my partner
- I get too easily irritated with my kids
- My sister / brother and I argue all the time
- I constantly feel pressure at my work.
- My boss is too critical
- My kid's habits get on my nerves

After you have identified your problem areas, find the ways to improve the most important relationships within your life.

Write a list of actions. For Example:

- Make a point not to argue with your parents next time you see them – let this be a conscious exercise

- Let your partner know that s/he is too critical and that her/his criticism is too destructive for you

- When you criticize someone make sure that your criticism is constructive

- Socialize with people that have similar interests to you and **deepen your friendships**

- Make a point to stop judging and blaming yourself. Change what you need to change but do not keep on worrying about your attitudes

CONSCIOUS PARENTING   MODULE 7 RELATIONSHIPS   IDENTIFY RELATIONSHIP PATTERNS

Date_____   Name_____

Relationship Patterns	Emotional Consequence	Positive Alternative / Action Items

EXERCISE 1: TEN TINY CHANGES

This exercise is designed to strengthen the connection you have within your family and to develop the understanding of other human beings that share your heart, your home, your life.

Introduce ten tiny changes within the world of your relationship habits, beliefs or actions.

Record and remember 10 particular habits that occur within your relationship:

- With your parents
- With your siblings
- With your friends
- With your partners

For example:

- Your obsession to keep a particular door open at all times,
- The habit to go to the same place for croissant every day,
- Your habit to wear the same lipstick,
- Your habit to read the newspapers at the table,
- Your habit to say the exact same things to your children before they go to school,
- Your habit to do the exact same thing to your partner before s/he goes to work (a kiss, or no kiss, a hug, or no hugs)
- Squeeze the tooth-brush in exact the same way.

You get the point, identify any weird and wonderful habit that we all secretly and sub-consciously worship.

Change them and do them in a different way. Surprise your partner, friends, parents or children. Try to please other members of your family.

You can do it: secretly, openly or discreetly. Do not say to your partner what are the habits, patterns that you have changed, or that you are working on. The examples of these little treats for your family could be:

- Help your partner or child with the house chores. Do something that is usually done by the other family member. If a mum is the one to cook at all times, the son might decide to take this task; if it is the mother washes the clothes, father might decide to take this task for a moment.

- Buy a present to the family member, with no particular reason, buy some flowers, or socks to your dad.

- Prepare a bath for the tired partner, just when you know s/he is returning from a difficult day at work.

- Pick up your spouse from a day of work if she usually uses public transport to commute to and back from work, or go for your kids after school if they usually use the school bus to commute.

At the end of the week take some time to discuss the 'tiny' changes. Did you recognize the little presents that you have received during the week? How did you recognize the presents and how did you feel receiving these gifts to your patterns, habits and the way of life.

If you did not recognize the gifts, ask yourself why did this happen? What is it that I need to do differently so that my family member will recognize that I have changed something. With these ten tiny changes, you will challenge the Master of Habits within your Mind that rules your Relationships and start exercising your Will Power towards more Love, Tolerance and Beauty within your life.

We also continue practicing Self-Remembering.

EXERCISE 2: ARE YOU TRULY LISTENING?

Ask yourself this question and stop for a moment to analyze your attitude towards the art of listening.

Do you like listening to others speak and encourage them to speak? Are you equally attentive to a friend, a neighbor, or a stranger. Do you focus on what the person is saying and are you cleat about the quality of conversation that you are having? Do you often interrupt the person who is speaking?

Use this exercise while you are trying to improve the relationships within your life. Active listening can do wonders. Also, active listening will save you from a big Time Waster called Gossiping.

Be aware of Gossiping.   Do not Gossip.

There are so many other inspiring things to talk about than Talking About Other People…

RULES OF ACTIVE LISTENING
- keep quiet when the other one is talking
- ask related questions and listen to the answers
- show compassion whether with a stranger, neighbor or your shop-keeper

Mindful Being   by Nuit

We train ourselves all through our life **to waste energy** following **our inner narratives**. We are often **unconsciously driven** by our fears, worries and fantasies. Enter the space of **Awareness** of the **present moment** with no emotional filters, no regrets nor hopes, no daydreaming and no nightmares.

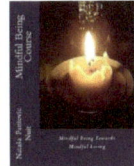

www.artof4elements.com

EXERCISE 3 EXERCISE CONSCIOUS SPEECH

EXERCISE 3A CHOSE A SUBJECT TO DEFEND OR ARGUE ABOUT DURING THE DAY

Chose a subject you usually get emotional about and de-touch from the feeling while you are defending your argument.

Stay behind the feeling.

Observe it. Check the physical sensation of it.

Is it in the stomach? Or in the chest?

Or perhaps it comes from the inspiration centre – from your throat?

Now, stop in the middle of your argument. Stop before you have finished it, let it go, no matter how passionate about it you might be.

Observe what happens to your body while you are exercising this conscious speech exercise.

Spiritual Journey Learn to Listen to Your Soul

Body Mind Soul
Train Love   Train Willpower
Respect Gaia   Respect Life
Respect Silence
Conscious Living
Mindful Eating   Mindful Being
Conscious Relationships

Alchemy of Love
Mindfulness Training

Exercise 3B Defend Somebody Else Point of View

Defend somebody else point of view even though you generally disagree with it.

Check how it feels to have the other person's point of view, argue it, defend it, work with it consciously.

Exercise 3C Stop in the middle of an argument

If you argue with somebody today, stop in the middle of the argument.

Let it go. Do not follow it any longer. Do not pursue it. Do not be right today.

Exercise 3D For and Against

Choose an argument that you often have with your partner or with your kids. For example: should I or not socialize with Mr. X; should I or not stay that late out with friends.

When you chose an argument, change the roles. Stay in the role of your child letting the child takes your role. Let the child lead the discussion. This is not an easy exercises, because we as parents, have a natural tendency to lead. Consciously, let the child lead the discussion. You will learn many interesting things through this play. Never abuse what you have learned through this 'play' because you will not be able to use this tool again.

When you are listening to your child acting the role of a parent, listen very carefully to the words spoken, you will hear lots of your-own words, but just in a way that your child understood them. Was this how you intended them? Or did they get lost within the 'translation' process within our brains?

Also, be conscious of your feelings, while the child is talking to you. What are the buttons your child is pushing and why are you reacting in a certain way?

At the end of discussion, ask for solutions so that you can get out of this exercises with a possible solution to the problem in question.

This exercise is here to highlight the 'untruthful' words that might become a problem within any communication, the unconscious speech that we all sometimes use.

We might be using words that are too strong or difficult to handle such as:

'you are stupid', 'you do not know!', 'you can not do it!' 'you are an idiot' etc.

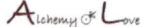
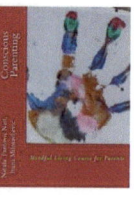

'All **conscious parents** hope that they will further develop:
- **Self-control** over thoughts and actions
- **Open Heart** protected by inner strength
- **Free Mind** to stay in-tuned with the new experiences
- An ability to stay **true to decisions** and follow them
- An increased capability for **Love**, **Wisdom** and **Peace**'

All of these statements come from our (human) unconsciousness and unfortunately leave an imprint on the mind, and might become a core belief later on in life. We inherited them from our parents, they are firmly engraved within our unconscious patterns and very often unwillingly we are passing them down to our children. Practicing Mindfulness we try to understand / get out of the magic circle of unconscious behavior. For our-own and Humanity sake: Let's try and stay conscious of our words.

Tasks:

- T1 Meditate in the morning – learn to get in touch with silence within yourself

- T2 Set your clock ½ hour earlier and write a page of stream-of-consciousness writing. From today, do it every day for the next 6 weeks

- T3 **Spiritual Company**

Exercise 4: Secret Gift

This exercise is designed to help you as a family learn more about yourself, work as a group, and express your feelings. You will together get inspired, get closer, you will feel that you belong to the family.

You will need a few envelopes. You can create your own envelopes together, and use this as an art exercise just before you start this lovely exercise.

Each member of the family writes his or her name on an envelope.

Each one of you should write a beautiful message to each of other members of your family. Messages could be poems, inspiring words, beautiful descriptions, quotes. You can add to the message a flower, a drawing, a little present, a collage of photos or a cookie, anything that comes to your mind that might bring a smile to your family member. You will prepare yourself for this exercise. Give yourself as much time as you wish, a day or two, three or a week. Have an appointment set to exchange your secret envelopes. The subject of your message should be: love, inspiration, life. They can be as philosophical or as simple as you wish them to be.

During your appointment, when you open your gifts, have a moment of silence. Before you exchange your reactions, write down your feelings, your thoughts, your reactions. After you had a moment to reflect, share with others, one by one, the content of the envelope and your thoughts, wishes, feelings. Enjoy the exercise and repeat once in awhile.

Mindful Being

'Our **mind** is constantly busy with thoughts and feelings about **our past, present or future**. To stop it from **useless chat**, we must learn how to hear this noise, become **aware of it**, and transform it through **concentration into mindfulness**.'

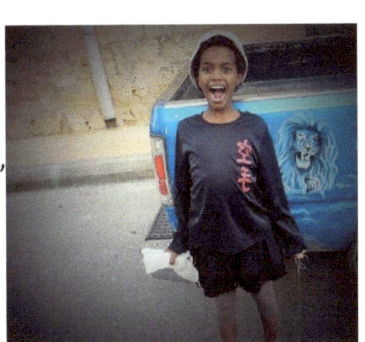

EXERCISE 5: CIRCLE OF LOVE

HOW WELL DO WE KNOW EACH OTHER

This exercise is designed to inspire you to get to know each other. Often we believe that we know things about our family members, and we take some basics for granted. This questionnaire will help you get closer to one another, you will start thinking about the other family member and you will become more harmonious as a group.

Take an empty piece of paper and ask a number of questions. Answer the questions for yourself, for your partner, and for each of your family members. The questionnaire should look like the following table:

Question	My	My Partners	Kid 1	Kid 2
Favourite colour				
Favourite book				
Favourite poem				
Favouring meal				
Favourite flower				
Favourite crystal				
Favourite animal				
Favourite sport				
Biggest Fear				
Biggest Love / Inspiration				
Strongest Fun				
How to relax				
The best quality				
What do I do when I am happy				
What do I do when I am sad				
What others do when I am happy				
What others do when I am sad				
1 thing I would like to change				

Compare your notes and discuss them in a circle of love. Circle of love has a rule that you can not criticize anybody's answers, you can not fight, you can not argue.

Circle of love is accepting, full of understanding, giving and loving.

EXERCISE 6: LEARN ABOUT EACH OTHER AND HAVE FUN

These exercises are designed to inspire you and strengthen a bond with the family members. They are fun and they will teach you about your loved ones through game and play. You can chose to exercises any of them during the week.

Exercise 6A: Our Story

This exercise is designed to strengthen the bond between family members. It is fun and it can be done at any time.

Narrate a story together.

Each member of the family should narrate the story for about minute or so. The order of story tellers is set in advance and it is respected all through the act. Act out your words while you speak, dance, use any props at hand (scarves, stones, flowers). Let the story flow and change from one narrator to the other. The story should last around 15minutes or if you like the experience, enjoy it and do it as long as you wish. You can record the performance either by a sound recorder or a camera.

Each family member should have a turn to give a subject to the story and to start the story giving it an initial look and feel. Have fun doing it!

Exercise 6B Punishment and Reward

Sorry wrong book! We don't respect this way of treating kids and we do not believe that reward and punishment should be a part of any family's routine and a way of life.

Exercise 6C Dance with your favorite music

Once a week dance together. Each one of you should get his or her own a choice of music and you can mix them together for ½ an hour fun.

It is good to start with a dance that is not too fast nor too slow, to warm up, to have a very fast and rhythmic melody somewhere at the middle of the session and to end with a meditative piece of music where you all respect the meditative mode of the dance.

There is one rule within this ½ hour, you should not talk between yourself. Just dance and enjoy yourself!

Exercise 6D Children on lead

Young children often stop to explore environment around them instead of following our past of walk. When walking with your children you can chose to have a lead or a push chair and to limit your child's movements or to run with your child playing whatever game the kid wants to be a part of. Run or collapse is an interesting exercise that encourages you to follow your child's rhythm for a moment, to run after the child, to rest when the rest is needed, to explore the flowers that surround you or just play with stones, waves and water. Be a child and play. Pay respect to the child within you and to your children.

Exercise 6E The Tree of Life

Chose a tree within your house and use it within this exercises.

Each one of the family members will create leafs from a colorful paper. write on the paper a wish.

Each paper should contain a quality each one of you would like to develop during the next 3 months. The papers will stay on the tree and they will be an inspiration for the family members to give secret gifts to each person.

The gifts would be poems or quotes or images that relate to the quality the family member has chosen. For example if the quality you would like to develop is love, you could photograph the person in the state of love and include this photo within the bunch of messages that are on the tree. After three months get together and discuss the messages and the little secret gifts.

Exercise 6F A hug, a kiss, a cuddle

Include an extra hug or an extra kiss or an extra cuddle into your routine of kisses, hugs and cuddles. Consciously try it out for a month and see will this become your habit later on in life.

Exercise 6G Family Melody

Create a family melody that each one of the family members know as your family 'whistle'. Use it to call your kids to join you or to find our where they are.

Use the family melody as a sign of recognition.

Exercise 6H Family Album

Print out your favorite photos and do an album of photos.

It is important that you physically print the photos out. This helps create a sense of family belonging that is very important.

You can also create collages and frame them as one painting. The collage could have a theme like: travels or growing up or our pats, etc.

Exercise 6I If I am an animal I would be _____

With this exercise we encourage a child to think and talk about his qualities allowing his or her imagination to rain this little game.

We ask the child to chose an animal that represents him, to chose an animal that attracts him.

Ask the child to write down 3-4 qualities that describe the animal and the resons why these qualities fascinate him or her.

Ask the child to draw the animal, to act as this animal

It is important to talk about the qualities of the animal in details…

You could buy a doll or a sculpture of that animal and give it as a present to your child.

If this is an animal that can be your pet, buy it and let your child develop a beautiful relationship with it.

As a continuation of this exercises write also down:

If I am a stone I would be _____

If I am a color I would be _____

If I am a flower I would be _____

If I am a musical instrument I would be _____

Make the above statements a subject of discussion allowing your child to tell you little secrets about his/her aspirations, worries, life.

Exercise 6G Stop and start from the beginning

If you started your day with anger or you have reacted the wrong way, it is never too late to stop and start it from the beginning. So if your child was telling you a story and an 'unexpected fight' happened, stop and start it again, from the point when your child is reading you the story.

Mindful Being   by Nuit

When we say **Mind** we think of: **consciousness**, awareness, cognitive thinking; but also of: **intuition**, subconscious gibberish, or **unconscious strata** influencing our lives. The 'state' of this **Mind**, our **positive** or **negative** attitude towards the world, is closely related to our experiences of **happiness** or **suffering**.

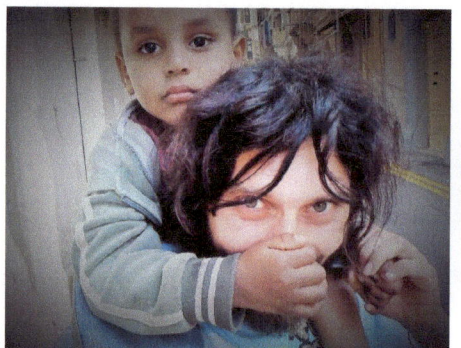

www.artof4elements.com

Exercise 7: Your Relationship Plan

We should devote time to talk about our relationship, our true needs, and goals, what are the empowering things within the relationship that we are grateful for, and what we would like to change so that the relationship becomes stronger and more beautiful.

Take a note-book with your partner and spend some time answering the questions separately.

We are starting with the True Goals and True Purpose to keep your focus on what is really important.

- My ultimate Spiritual goal in life is:

    o   For example: happiness as a state-of-being;
    o   oneness with God
    o   lightness of Being, etc.

- My purpose in Life is:

    o   For example: to stay inspired and to inspire others
    o   to live peacefully and stay healthy
    o   to be in love with the world, etc.

- My mission in Life is:

    o   For example: To reach my highest potential in everything I do
    o   To raise my children as inspired and loving adults
    o   To see God in all, etc.

- I wish to share my skills and beliefs with the World through:

    o   For example: Giving Yoga Classes
    o   Writing a book of poetry
    o   The positive example to my kids and friends, etc.

- 5 most important things in my life are:

    o   For example: Freedom, Love, Knowledge, Family and Friends; Union with God in meditation, prayer, etc.

What are the things I appreciate most in my relationship?

Where do I see this relationship going? What is our future?

What would I like to be able to do while in this relationship?

Body

- Walk the dogs together in the morning
- Have time to jog on my own in the afternoons

Emotions

- Develop an ability to cope with feelings openly and lovingly
- Avoid jealousy attacks
- Be truthful and honest about my feelings, needs, wants (devote time for sharing thoughts and feelings)

Thoughts

- wish to go back to school to acquire new business skills
- we could learn a new language together to add fun to our lives

Soul

- Devote space and time to developing deeper friendships
- Join a mantra singing or a prayer or a meditation group
- Take drawing classes on my-own / together to enhance creativity

What would I like to keep or change within this relationship?

- more time to be on my-own
- more time to do inspiring things together
- more freedom in my relationships with others
- wish you are not so critical / sarcastic, let's practice Positive Feedback together
- wish to have more time on my own while you are with the children

An addiction could become the number one value in our life. Many lose things that are extremely important to their addictions to food, drinking, work, drugs, sex, gambling, shopping, etc.

Write down this sentence:

- If you would quit _____, I would be able to _____.

While analyzing the questions and answers together, be open and honest, work with the essence, don't let the trivial distract you. For example, have you ever heard a statement...

- If I had more money, I could holiday more often. Then I could spend more quality time with my family and friends

In this statement, the problem is not money, but the luck of quality time together. Find ways to enhance your time together.

At the end of the exercise, create a list of concrete actions that are a result of this exchange with your partner and add them to your Life.

Repeat this exercise every 6 months or a year.

EXERCISE 8: EXPRESS FREEDOM

This exercise is here so that we can express our gratitude towards the quality of FREEDOM. Even within a relationship we should still have our 'breathing space', we should still experience a 'sense of freedom', and enjoy 'doing things on our own'.

Compose an aria with a title 'Freedom'

Write a poem with a subject 'Freedom'

Draw a painting called 'Freedom'

Plan and execute a Freedom day in a month or in a week.

EXPRESS LOVE

Compose an aria with a title 'Love   Write a poem with a subject 'Love

Draw a painting called 'Love. Plan and execute a Love day in a month or in a week.

Come Back to Love   Come Back to Love

Transformation Tools Conscious Parenting

Module 8 Our Greater Surrounding

Understand Conscious Relationships

We live in our greater surrounding and when we become conscious and aware, our capability for love grows and expands into our surroundings – Earth, animals, plants, strangers

QUESTIONNAIRE 1 OUR GREATER SURROUNDING

This questionnaire contains a number of words that describe your attitude to your greater surrounding, your attitude towards Earth, animals, strangers.

Read each item and rate them from 1 (lowest) to 5 (highest). Answer to what extent you feel this way right now, that is, at the present moment.

- I take care of Earth because we are too nature
- I recycle, I use as little plastic as possible, I eat organics, I am vegetarian, etc.
- I am grateful for every day and I express my thanks to people that surround me
- I love animals and take care of them whenever I can
- I am never too busy to help a friend
- I support various NGOs in their work to help Earth, Animals, Poor
- I am active in my Local Council, my Building Council working on the better environment
- I actively support environmental protection initiatives
- I help in my children School's voluntary activities
- I try to understand rather than judge people who are accused of being wrong

WRITE THE ANSWERS OF THE PERSONALITY QUESTIONNAIRE

Conscious Parenting   Module 8 Greater Surrounding   Questionnaire 1

Date_____   Name_____

Our Greater Surrounding	1-5
I take care of Earth because we are too nature	
I recycle, I use as little plastic as possible, I eat organics, I am vegetarian, etc	
I am grateful for every day and I express my thanks to people that surround me	
I love animals and take care of them whenever I can	
I am never too busy to help a friend	
I support various NGOs in their work to help Earth, Animals, Poor	
I am active in my Local Council, my Building Council working on the better environment	
I actively support environmental protection initiatives	
I help in my children School's voluntary activities	
I do charity work	

My List of Priorities: Items Marked as 1, 2 and 3 are:

Our Greater Surroundings		1	2	3

After you have answered your questions, meditate on answers and where the problems within your life might be. Use a colored marker to highlight areas that might need improvement. Add whatever you feel is missed out from this list.

The ranking from 1 to 5 will indicate your list of priorities.

ACTION ITEM FROM THE PERSONALITY QUESTIONNAIRE

Study each answer that you are not happy with and determine what precise action you would like to do to change your attitude toward our grater surrounding.

Write down the areas that need improvement. Be specific…

For example:

- I very much wish to be kind, loving and giving to my fellow human beings but the opportunity never shows up
- I am too busy to join any NGO
- The world is too f…ked up that an individual effort is useless
-

Change these into positive attitudes and create A WORLD OF YOUR DREAMS

EXERCISE 1 CHANGE THE WORD

Within this exercise you will write answers on the following questions about the environment and your relationship with Gaia.

I like animals because _____

I like plants because _____

I think that Earth is _____

If my friend dirty the environment I would _____

When people smoke next to me, I tell them _____

When I think of healthy nutrition I think of _____

When I think about health the most important is that I_____

When I think of a healthy planet, we would need to _____

When I think of happy animals I think of _____

You can change the world

Exercise 2 | I have the power to change the world

If you have a possibility to open an NGO, what is the NGO that you would create?

Would you work on your own or with your friends, what type of activity would you include within the work of such an organization; what are the areas that your NGO would cover?

If you have a power to change anything you want, what would you do:

- Adopt a Child
- Clean the Planet
- Plant Trees
- Grow Your Organics

Create a list of actionable items that can easily become your reality.

- get a plot of land or grow your own veggies on your roof
- become a member of an NGO that works with deforestation
- teach your children to give a part of their pocket money for a charity
- help a grandma from your neighborhood...

For children: Give your child a following scenario:

If somebody has decided to cut the forest next to your home, what would that mean to you, your friends, your pets, the living being in the forest. Ask your child to describe all the negative effects of such an act and ask him to analyse what's why's of such happenings.

Ask your child, 'if you have the power to do something about it, what exactly would you do?

How can such an activity be stopped?'

Let the child's imagination go wild and allow all the impossible-s to happen.

This exercise is designed to create an awareness of all the things one can do to help protect our Mother Earth from destruction.

EXERCISE 2: SERVICE

Any act of service, performed in a spirit of unconditional giving, expands the qualities of compassion, love, and tolerance. You will learn to serve Divine through the people you are helping.

Make sure you help someone every day this week.

Be more attentive to other people's needs and you will see that there are many ways to help. Ask them do they need your help, or just go and do it.

Your service could be done for animals or environment you are living

in. We are all part of the same Life Force

Tasks:

Exercise 3: Your Children and Environment

Exercise 3A: Feed the Birds

Put some birds seeds in your plant pot or create a small bird feeder (you can use a coconut shell) and enjoy birds becoming regular visitors to your balcony, or garden.

This creates such joy for children.

Let them feed the birds and become their friends. You can use millet, sunflower seeds, cake crumbs, or bread crumbs to add to your birds seeds collection. Birds will also love a shallow bowl of water for drinking and bathing.

Exercise 3B: Create a Garden

Start from the very beginning of the process - get some fruit pips to sprout. Tell the kids to put some stones in the bottom of a clean jar and add a layer of compost. Once the seedling appears, and it has three or four leaves, your children can repot it into a small pot with compost. You could also try slicing off the top of carrots, placing them in a shallow dish of water and watch them sprout! Any seeds will also sprout.

Exercise 3C: Plant a Tree

Let your children collect some tree seeds - conkers from a chestnut tree, acorns from an oak tree, seeds from a palm tree. All trees produce seeds – so let them chose their variety. It is worth planting many seeds they collect, in case some don't work. Some need complex temperature conditions of frost and warmth to germinate, but let the Nature work and your children observe – it is a wonderful process.

God created **Nature**
Full of **Chaos**
Where no two things are **Equal**
Where no sound, no colour,
no shape is repeated.
Man copied God and created
Symmetry, **Mathematics**,
Music, Straight Lines
Man copied God and created
Perfection.
Together Man-made perfect elements create
an **Absolute Disorder**
Together God-made
imperfections result in an
Ultimate Harmony.

Perfection by **Nuit** Art of 4 Elements

EXERCISE 3D: PLANT VEGGIES

You can plant veggies in your garden or on your roof or balcony in the pots. Let your children dig the soil, mix the compost and play with Earth. Let the children do the watering, weeding, slug removing and picking! The garden will stay their creation – watch their wonder and beauty unfold!

This activity exercises patience, will power, expectations, and the understanding of the powers of Nature, because the plants sometimes need to be watered daily and sometimes could be very difficult to grow.

TRANSFORMATION TOOLS ONLINE LIFE COACHING

MODULE 9 YOUR DREAMS

Turn away from your dream and it will come back to you. Follow it and it will give you a tremendous amount of pleasure and learning.

Life is what we make of it.

Our dreams become our reality.

Our reality becomes the world we are all living in.

Addictions and habits do not support our Dreams. They bring us back to Instincts, Laziness, and they keep on ruining our health and wellbeing. They are usually very expensive.

Consumption of alcohol, drugs, smoking, impulsive shopping, over-eating, sugar addiction, eating too much junk food, wasting time on TV, computer games, laziness, worry, constant messaging , keeping unnecessary items instead of getting rid of them, lying for no reason, being a workaholic, etc. They all stay our little burdens that keep hold of our lives.

Getting rid of your instinctive behavior strengthens your willpower to change and to take responsibility within your life.

To help your child live his dreams listen to your child from the very early

age. Talk with Your Child

- About taboos
- About sex
- About gay couples
- From very early age teach them to ask questions: Who are we? What is the purpose of Life? Why are we here? What is God?
- About sickness and death.
- Allow your kids to answer any question, listen to them, you might learn something

Exercise 1 Identify Your True Dreams

Want - What is it exactly that you want / that are your priorities in life? What activities do I love to do in my free time? What is it that I loved doing before, as a kid or before I had kids?

For Your Body:

- Is it a sane mind, Is it a stronger body, Is it a healthier body
- Is it more money

For Your Mind

- Is it more love
- Is it less anger / hatred / struggle with fears
- Is it more time to play, be creative, laugh with friends

For Your Soul

- Do you know how to listen to your soul
- Do you meditate / pray
- Do you write, Do you draw, Do you dance

For Your Family

- Do you respect Rhythm
- Do you give enough space for Love
- Do you respect Freedom

EXERCISE 1A I PERFORM (UN)HAPPILY

This exercise should be done with your partner, if you have one.

Make a list of activities that you do willingly and happily and the list on the opposite side of the table that you do unhappily. For example you can put within your list things like: I do not like talking to anybody in the morning, I do not like when TV is on when I talk to somebody, I dislike when you read newspapers or answer your mobile when we eat together, I do not like cleaning after you.

You could try exchanging with your partner or with your children the activities that you perform unhappily.

If you do not like washing dishes consider exchanging this duty for any other your partner performs unhappily for a week.

Do have in mind that some of the 'chores' just simply need to be done and if you suffer doing them, perhaps you can find a way to do this activity 'mindfully'.

Can I change anything within this list?

EXERCISE 2 YOUR IMAGINARY LIVES

You will LOVE this one!

If you had a chance to do it all over again, to be re-born again, imagine the lives you would live. What would you be: a priest, a yogi, an actor, a male, a female, a businessman, a teacher, a healer, a scientist?

Write down whatever comes to your mind, whatever new circumstances excite you, whatever new successes would intrigue you, whatever qualities of these imaginary lives would inspire you.

This can be also done as an exercise where you imagine that you won $1,000,000. Staying without any financial pressures, give us a New World of Opportunities.

Try! You'll Love it!

QUESTIONNAIRE 1 YOUR TRUE DREAMS

Your True Dreams are within you. Your True Dreams could be reachable if you understand what they really are.

Answer to what extent do you feel this way right now.

- I have adequate time to do what I want in my life
- I have adequate finances to do what I want in my life
- I have adequate energy to do what I want in my life
- I have balance between work and leisure to fully participate in life
- I love spending time in nature and I have enough time and energy to do so
- Spirituality means lot to me and I spend enough time in my spiritual pursuits
- Achieving something valuable for my Soul _____ is the highest goal in life
- I am excited when I learn something new and I created time and space for new learning adventures
- I find the world to be a very interesting and inspiring place. I have fun exploring its wonders
- My work is productive and inspiring and my work environment is healthy
- I have a loving relationship with my friends and family. I spend enough time with them.
- I love horse-riding, drawing, football _____, and I created time and space for my passion
- What are priorities in an ideal healthy family? What are your family realities, priorities that you live at the moment? What are the priorities that you need to protect?
- Make a list of priorities that you would like to follow to have a healthy family with happy and inspired children.

ADD YOUR OWN QUESTIONS. WRITE THE ANSWERS OF THE PERSONALITY QUESTIONNAIRE

Conscious Parenting — Module 9 Your Dreams — Questionnaire 1

Date_____   Name_____

Your True Dreams

Your True Dreams	1-5
Time	
Energy	
Money	
Health	
Spirituality	
Happy Family	

My List of Priorities: Items Marked as 1, 2 and 3 are:

My True Dreams	1	2	3

ACTION ITEM FROM THE PERSONALITY QUESTIONNAIRE

Study each answer that you are not happy with and determine what precise action you would like to do to change your state of body, mind, emotions.

Write down the areas that need improvement. Be specific...

- More quality time with my family – family meal once a day
- Time to be silent, to read, to walk - wake up 1 hour earlier to meditate and do the soul's diary
- Create time for friends, for deeper contacts and meaningful socializing
- Develop my skills to successfully start working on my long term plans in life
- Creating time to express love through play and laughter

To achieve my highest potential and the highest potential of my family I will:

Be Specific: about time,

        quantity and

               quality of activity that will change

        your body, mind and

allow your soul to express fulfilling your highest potential.

While creating your action list for True Dreams to become your reality, have in mind two things:

GRATITUDE   Be grateful for what you already have

IMPROVEMENT   Constantly improve, learning new ways to Love and Be

Be creative, be honest. This list should now become your Action List. Do whatever you can to change uninspiring to inspiring, chaotic to harmonious, confused to balanced, irritated to loving...

CONSCIOUS PARENTING   MODULE 9 TRUE DREAMS   IDENTIFY TRUE DREAMS
Date_____   Name_____

Living my Dreams	Emotional Consequence	Positive Alternative / Action Items

QUESTIONNAIRE 2 YOUR CHILD'S DREAMS

SURVEY FOR CHILDREN

Read each item and rate them from 1 (lowest) to 5 (highest). Answer to what extent you feel this way right now, that is, at the present moment.

1. I love arts, music, dance.
2. I love narrating stories that I invent
3. I am curious and full of questions
4. I keep my word.
5. I make good judgments even in difficult situations.
6. I have good friends
7. I love sports
8. I wish to have more of .... In my life

Ask your child to write a story...

Imagine, what would you be in your imaginative life: an astronaut, an actor, a male, a female, a footballer, a scientist?

Let him / her write down whatever comes to his / her mind, whatever excites him / her, whatever inspires her / him.

This will be an interesting reading for all of you!

Tasks:

- T1 Meditate in the morning and get in touch with the silence within yourself

- T2 Write Your Soul's Diary

- T3 Repeat Mobile / Internet / TV off exercise

- T4 Check your Diet and Exercise Regime: Are you following your Module 1 Resolutions?

TRANSFORMATION TOOLS CONSCIOUS PARENTING

MODULE 10 YOUR TRUE GOALS

Create Reality of Your Dreams

Our True Goal Is To:

- ❖ Inspire, motivate, and encourage

What is Your?

To help you with your **True Goal** write down:

1. Who are the people I admire? What are their qualities and what is it that I admire? Write at least 7 names.

2. What is the book that left the most impression on me? Can the main characters tell me something about my Goals?

- What is it that touched me so deeply?
- What is it within me that resonate with the main message of the book
- What is the main learning that I am left behind

3. What is the film that inspired me most? What is the reason for it?

4. Is there a business or career that would help me do what I love to do?

5. Is there a hobby that I should keep that would help me do what I love to do?

Exercise 1   Your Personal Development Plan

A good self development plan is a journey, an ongoing process of personal development. Write your main skills, your main qualities, your main interest. Make a drawing of it, make it FUN and color each area as it first comes to your Mind. Your Soul will talk to you through Colors.

The following are the questions you need to answer to be able to build your personal development plan:

1. Where are you right now?
2. Where do you want to be?
3. What are your core strengths?
4. What are your Weaknesses / Improvement areas?
5. Write down your Core Beliefs…
6. What are your Short-Term Plans / Goals?
7. What are your Long-Term Goal? What is the purpose to which you wish to devote the rest of your life?
8. List a number of Short Term Actions / Milestones for achieving your Long Term Goal
9. What are your Goals and Actions for the next year?
10. What are your Goals and Actions for the longer term?

Create action steps: Small and Big Ones. These actions need not to be perfect, you will fine tune them as you go along.

Commitment: Discipline yourself to do your actions

Your action should be your **inspiration**. If you are happy and having fun, you take care of your Body, Mind and Soul, your creativity will flourish, and the end result will always be more fun and more happiness.

Doing something simply because everyone else is doing it, or because your loved ones think it is the best for you, will not help you to reach your highest potential. What is truly important to you as an individual, what flows with your strengths and weaknesses, what inspires you most? Be honest with the answers, seek clarity and your Soul will show you your purpose.

If your heart and your mind are not in-tuned they will become opposing forces within your life. The mind will constantly be saying, 'I have to do this now…' but your heart will stop it, saying: 'I am not enjoying this, let's leave it for tomorrow'. Within this game of opposites we will become lazy, over-loaded with work that we are not finishing, and we will end up feeling unhappy.

If we are using pure will-power to fight our heart, we will become tired very quickly, but if we are using our Heart's strengths, its inspiration, passion and calling, these two opposing forces will act in Union to produce SUPER results.

So, sit in a quiet place, go deep into your meditative state, and write, write whatever comes to your Mind. The answer that makes you feel inspired, peaceful and fulfilled is the one you are looking for.

Draw it! Have FUN with IT! Stick IT on your Kitchen Board! And NOW Live IT!

Tasks:

- T1 Meditation
- T2 Diet and Exercises
- T3 Give yourself Time for Creative Inspiration

Transformation tools Conscious Parenting

Module 11 Spirituality

What is Karma?

Exercise 1 What is Karma?

Karma is a set of actions and reactions that are interconnected, a set of cause and effects that form a Natural Universal Law and are operating in the realm of human life. A person is affected by his or her thoughts, emotions and actions.

Karma could be:

- National

- Inherited from parents

- Caused by a set of incarnations (if you believe in incarnations)

Each person's karma interacts, exchanges, influences each other

> 'For the only decree of **Karma** - an eternal and immutable decree - is absolute Harmony in the world of matter as it is in the world of Spirit. It is not, therefore, Karma that rewards or punishes, but it is we, who reward or punish ourselves according to whether we work with, through and along with nature, abiding by the laws on which that Harmony depends, or - break them.' (Secret Doctrine, Blavatsky)

> '**Karma**... One of the most important of the laws of nature. Ceaseless in its operation, it bears alike upon planets, systems of planets, races, nations, families, and individuals. It is the twin doctrine to reincarnation. So inextricably interlaced are these two laws that it is almost impossible to properly consider one apart from the other. No spot or being in the universe is exempt from the operation of Karma, but all are under its sway, punished for error by it yet beneficently led on, through discipline, rest, and reward, to the distant heights of perfection. It is a law so comprehensive in its sweep, embracing at once our physical and our moral being.' (Ocean Of Theosophy Ocean William Q. Judge p. 89)

Exercise 1 So What is Karma For You?

Exercise 2: Your Spiritual Diary

The **Spiritual Diary** let us focus our energies towards important things in our lives – creativity, virtues, righteousness, inspiring writings, spiritual company, God.

Spiritual Diary is a great help within the spiritual path.

Spiritual Diary is there to remind you of what is important and it is there so you can avoid the horrible time-wasters that keep occupying our hours / days / weeks / months – TV, Computer, Gossiping, Fearful Thinking – that keep us away from spending time within the creative flow.

You will keep the spiritual diary every day, continuously, for two months. This method was included within the teaching of many spiritual masters.

You will record the time spent in spiritual practices. Devoting regular time to the Spiritual Practices is an indication that your curiosity towards Spirit and your relationship with Spirit is widening and deepening.

The *spiritual diary* is very sacred. It should always be a true reflection of your inner state.

Spiritual Diary is there to help you identify problems and inspirations on your spiritual path. After some time, you will answer the questions such as: Is my meditation improving? Is my capacity for love growing? Is my self-confidence increasing? Do I allow myself enough creative time to be able to flourish?

If your day is truly disappointing and you realize that you lied and cheated and wasted your time and energy, you will stay aware of this fact and will change tomorrow. If you told lies today, don't tell them tomorrow. This is very simple!

When you keep diary, you practice the attention. We remember only if our attention is there, only if we are awake. That is why we do not remember what we've done only a week ago, how did we spend our days.

Spiritual & Creative Diary   **Month........**

Questions   Dates

Physical Body

When did wake up?

When did I go to sleep?

Mark for your sleep / dream

What is the physical exercise that I've done?

- walking
- running
- any individual or collective sport

Mark for your physical activity today

Food & Drink Quality

Food & Drink Quantity

Mark for your nutritional intake

Mindful Eating   by Nuit

'Become **Mindful** of your food. Your enjoyment will multiply. The **quality** will replace the **quantity**, **Awareness** will become your guide and protector. With the **awareness** you will start **respecting yourself**.'

with Delicious RAW VEGAN RECIPES

www.artof4elements.com

Spiritual & Creative Diary   Month........

Questions   Dates

Mental Body

How long did I meditate

- in the morning, during the day, in the evening

What is the noise level around me (noise from TV, Radio, etc.)

Did I read any spiritual book today?

Did I spend time with the wise and inspiring people?

Did I do any selfless service today?

How much time have I spent in a creative activity?

- Writing
- Drawing, Story Telling

How much time did I spend in nature / with nature

Spiritual & Creative Diary   Month……..

Questions   Dates

Emotional Body

How much time did I spend with friends / loved ones in a good quality exchange

Have I made love today, or have I fallen into sex today

Time spent with useless company / activity

- Gossiping, TV / Games / Social Media
- Worrying, fighting, arguing

Time spent doing nothing / worrying

My Children

Quality time spent with my children

Did I follow the routine vs. freedom with my children today?

Shouting, screaming, scolding

Laughing, playing, exploring

My Soul

What are the virtues that I am developing consciously?

Non Violence

Truthfulness

Lightness of being – healthy humor

Love

Prayer

TRANSFORMATION TOOLS CONSCIOUS PARENTING

MODULE 12 SPIRITUALITY & YOU
Gratefully Giving & Receiving Divine Flow

Exercise 1 Have Divine as the Main Focus All Through Your Day

Just before you start walking, talking, driving, just before you open a door, or start an activity, have in mind that everything is Divine, that all is One, that All is God. Put this thought consciously in front of all your activity.

You are an Instrument in God's Hands

Feel all through the day the interconnectedness of all beings, all things, all actions, all thoughts, all feelings. Remember all through the day the synchronicity that exists in all our lives. Remind yourself that you are an instrument in God's Hands, an instrument of Divine...

Divine in day-to-day tasks

One of your daily tasks should be done with love, enthusiasm and devotion as though your life depends on it. Whether you chose to clean your bedroom, wash the dishes or wash your car in this way, do it completely, engage fully, do it the best you can.

Exercise 2 Drumming, Meditation, Yoga Circle

Join a drumming circle, a meditation circle or start going to yoga.

Sing mantras and devotional songs... Singing is **healing**

Sing songs that are inspiring, that are created to help humankind or a personal growth.

Feeling the vibration of the sound is a sacred and profound experience. It is a form of Bhakti Yoga. It needs the proper breathing, proper relaxation, and proper state of mind. Chanting properly, your being starts to shine, your soul finds the way to express itself through sounds and your heart opens.

Through the chanting we develop our relationship with

Divine Join a Mantra Chanting Circle or a Drumming Circle!

Indigenous cultures practiced circle drumming for thousands of years. If you can not join a Drumming Circle in your neighborhood, form your own Circle, join together with friends and explore the magic of jamming. Respect the sacredness of the drumming rituals. Drumming is a healing force. Clear your mind and surrender to the divine beat. The drums will do the healing.

How to chant?

Chanting, your body becomes a temple and an instrument. Respect your body signals. Are you nervous when you chant? Is your voice very quiet, are you afraid to be seen or heard? Is your throat too tight? Are you **chanting** from your navel or from your head? Are you centered, grounded, balanced and do you respect equally the needs of your heart and the needs of your head? Are you too loud? Is your ego fighting to get in? Do you chant because you want others to hear you or because you want to become the Divine energy and you want to let the Divine flow run through you.

Exercise 3 Enter Your Dream World

Out of Body Awareness

Dreams are a **symbolic represent**ation of what is going on in our **waking consciousness**.

Dreams also represent the **collective unconscious** that might be common to all cultures and

Dreams are also our ability to view the spiritual world.

For **Jung**, the symbolic messages contained in our dreams are the way to integrate the **archetypal forces** into our **existence**. For Steiner, we go into the dreamtime or spiritual world in order to find our true self.

In either way, by deepening our **awareness** of dream states we deeper connect with the states that are behind our **ordinary thinking and sense perception**.

Our soul can absorb the spiritual truths during sleep. You could decide to consult your dreams or to follow your intuitive soul.

Practice Separating from your Body

The following exercise is designed to practice separating from the body.

While meditating, sitting cross legged, or laying down, imagine that your head starts turning left or right. Follow it. Feel it turning. See within your mind's eye the room changing – you are observing a left side of the room and then the right side. If you are laying down, practice a slow movement up within your imagination with the whole of your body. Then, practice slow turning around the centre within your stomach.

DREAMS & PRACTICING AWARENESS

Just before falling asleep give your 'Self' an instruction to remember the dream and to become aware of the 'Self' within the dream.

Before falling asleep say 'I will become conscious of my astral journey'.

If you had an interesting dream the night before, say to yourself that you wish to continue with the dream or repeat the dream you had.

Or: 'I wish to help somebody this night',

Or: 'I wish to dream of _____'

REMEMBERING DREAMS

Your Dream Diary

Another DIARY? OH, NOOOOO! This is only for the courageous few! Set your alarm clock at 3:45AM (not joking!) and wake up to write down your dreams. For the parents with babies this might be their baby's scream alarm clock, yet for the rest of us experiment a few times. Put a note-book on your bed-side table for the least disturbance and when you wake up, write down the notes of your dreaming state.

Try to answer the following questions:

- was your dream in color
- did you have a beautiful dream or a nightmare
- what is the feeling you are left behind: inspired, elevated, scared, confused
- write down the dream if you remember it, or just parts of it that 'feel'
- important how active, expressive, alive were you in your dreams is there a
- message you are left with after this dream

Watch out for **powerful dreams** with intense feelings, intricate symbols and strong colors. A dream could become a spiritual force, a message from your **Soul**, if we just learn how to dream with **awareness**, or how to stay 'awake' while sleeping.

In the morning, **connect with your dream** and try to 'feel' it, its meaning and its message.

EXERCISE 4 SEEK SPIRITUAL COMPANY

Once you have embarked on the journey of spiritual discoveries, you will seek inspiration from people around you – you will seek **philosophers**, **artists**, **yogis**, **gurus** and friends that will discuss spiritual topics with you.

Good spiritual books are great companions on a **spiritual journey**. Check our List of Recommended Spiritual Literature.

Tasks:

- T1 Meditate in the morning

- T2 Write your spiritual diary in the evening practicing self-remembering, recalling the events of the day in reverse

- T3 Be Happy. The Lightness of Being is the Most Important Exercise of them all!

Will and Love Practiced to invoke her Majesty **Kundalini**
In the world where **Adepts** die & bloom as **Lotuses**
The perfection of Union is **Silence**
The **Desire for Beauty** within a **Dolphin**
that possesses the **Soul**
keeping it **under Abyss,** giving It **Madness of the Pan**
seeking the **totality of all possible 'do'-s**
jumping into the river full of **streams of thoughts**
Until... The steady sound of a flute **Stills Its Mind**
Freeing it from its Grossness and Violence
destroying the **illusions** of shame and desires,
and loathsome forms of **Ego-structures**
allowing **Faun to appear and Accept Its True Nature**
Aiming at **Perfection** day after day Purging all of 'I's,
Uniting with 'All'
the **Will** finally becomes the **Self**
the **Faun transforms into the Unicorn**
that knows the **Life of Pure Joy**
and have **only thoughts of clarity and splendour**
Worshiping Silence Ecstasy Transcends Expression
The **Soul** is **Freed**

Alchemy of Soul by Nuit

artof4elements.com

List of Recommended Books

1. Tao Te Ching
2. **Patanjali** Yoga Sutras (The Light of the Soul, Alice Bailey)
3. Bhagavad-Gita (with **Sivananda's** commentary)
4. **Ouspensky**, The Fourth Way
5. **Sri Aurobindo**, The Synthesis of Yoga
6. **C.W. Leadbeater**, Invisible Helpers; Man Visible and Invisible; Chakras
7. **Powel**: Astral Body; Ethetic Body; Mental Body
8. **Shivananda**: Kundalini Yoga; Concentration and Meditation
9. Swami **Devananda**: Meditation and Mantras
10. **Avalon**: Serpent Power
11. **Krishnamurti's** Collection of Writings
12. **Aleister Crowley**: The Book of Thoth
13. **Theresa of Avila**: the Interior Castle
14. **Steiner**: How to know higher words;
15. Tibetan Book of Living and Dieing
16. **Yogananda**: Autobiography of a Yogi
17. **Alice Bailey**: The Light of the Soul
18. **C.G. Jung**: The Psychology of Kundalini Yoga
19. **Herman Hesse**: Collection of Writings
20. **Shrii Shrii Anandamurti**: Collection of Writings
21. **Makaja**: Kundalini
22. **Dalai Lama**: Destructive Emotions
23. **Osho Rajneesh**: Book of Secrets
24. Tolstoy: Collection of Writings
25. I Ching
26. Kabbalah
27. Mythology, Symbols and Signs
28. Astrology

Our Children

Shifting Education goals

Knowledge as a dynamic entity

One of the biggest problems of education today is that the 'factory model' of teaching: the top-down approach and the rewards-and-punishments approach, limit students' ability to contribute with their imagination and creativity.

The system needs a shift in focus: from one that teaches children a curriculum, to the one that inspires lifelong learning. Education has to shift from conveying knowledge in a static curriculum package to enabling teachers and students to view knowledge as a dynamic entity that is constantly changing.

Alternative Educational Models

Both Waldor and Montessori learning methods establish a collaborative environment without tests, with the child's learning and **creativity** at the centre of the focus. They go against the grain of traditional educational methods.

Some students who experienced such schooling went on to launch revolutionary business models.

Larry Page and Sergei Brin, both ex-Montessori students, launched Google. Amazon's marketing strategy, designed by ex-Montessori student Jeff Bezos, involves 'planting seeds' in people's heads to buy their desired books.

What these people also have in common is the ability to develop simple but ingenious ideas into extraordinary profitable projects.

The Finns are the current leaders of **educational reform**. In the **Finish educational model**, active learning and 'holistic' development is taken seriously. In Finland, school-children do not sit at their desks memorising; they walk around their places gathering information or discussing ideas in work-groups.

Their schools are an extension of their homes. Students share responsibility to undertake tasks. They take care of the school's pet tortoises and fish, they water the plants, help in the library, empty wastepaper baskets and recycle waste and keep the school yard clean. They also help in the school kitchen and in the distribution of lunch.

New Educational Goals

The 'rightful' goal of education should be to help children bring out and expand their talents and learn how to live to the full their mental, emotional and physical potential.

Waldorf schools follow this **'integral' approach** to develop a child's physical, mental, emotional and spiritual capacities. In such schools children are fully involved in each lesson: their thinking hat is constantly on, they fully connect with the subject matter, they are inspired, and the learning approach fully stimulates their curiosity.

Communication between teachers and students is shifted from following commands to engaging in conversation that helps students discover new methods and solve problems. Education is aimed to help children develop their interaction with the world, teaching them how to ask appropriate questions, how to analyse a problem, stimulating a desire to learn, and flexibility to consider different viewpoints.

Since we live in the world of constant changes, our children should be constantly exploring play, innovation, and developing imagination as a cornerstone of learning.

Knowledge is fluid and evolving, and we need to set in play the cultural viewpoint that acknowledges this constant change and evaluates creativity as the base of the new world they will be creating.

Will we learn from Finland?

Educational Lessons from Finland
Test oriented culture

One of the unfortunate limitations of test-oriented is that if children pass their school tests, they are considered winners; otherwise, they are viewed as losers and this classification is engraved in their minds at a very young age.

In an exam-driven culture, a good student means one who achieves high scores. In such a system, life skills such as self-confidence, contemplation, passion for science and love for knowledge are all underestimated. **Education is just a passive reproduction of the ideas others have presented. Children** are encouraged to simply repeat; they are spoon-fed, even though this method is boring.

Educational Lessons from Finland = Finland and no exams policy

Finland, a current leader of educational reform in the world, has implemented a no-national-exams policy and succeeded in creating a generation of inspired and outstanding students.

At the same time it is committed to **quality teaching**; to teach in Finland, one needs to have a master's degree.

The Programme for International Student Assessment (Pisa) measures average scores for reading, mathematics and science literacy by country. Finnish students have continued to place close to the top of all the subjects on the Pisa list; by comparison, the US ranked 15th in read-ing, 19th in maths and 27th in science.

Finland's no-national-exams policy goes against the trend of competition, standardisation, testing and control. The education authorities were criticised by traditional forces; they were warned that the end of tracking was a recipe for mass mediocrity.

However, after examining the Finish educational model, Linda Darling-Hammond, Professor of Education at Stanford University, US, commented: "Thirty years ago, Finland's education system was a mess.

"It was quite mediocre, very inequitable. It had a lot of features our system has: very top-down testing, extensive tracking, highly variable teachers, and they managed to reboot the whole system."

Pasi Sahlberg, of Finland's Education Department, explained: "We prepare children to learn how to learn, not how to take a test".

He noted that even the concept of Pisa goes against Finland's no exam policy, adding that "we are not much interested in Pisa. It's not what we're about."

EDUCATIONAL LESSONS FROM FINLAND - FINISH EDUCATIONAL SECRETS OF SUCCESS
Dr Sahlberg said Finnish children don't start school until they are seven years old because it is seen as a **violation of children's right to be children** for them to start school any sooner than seven. "The first six years of education are not about academic success," he said. "We don't measure children at all. It's about being ready to learn and finding your passion."

According to the most recent survey by the Organisation for Economic Co-operation and Development (OECD) the smallest differences in the world between the strongest and weakest students are found in Finland. There are no private schools in Finland; all the schools are public.

Since 1985, **Finnish students are not tracked or grouped by ability**. Since 1991, Finnish authorities have also stopped holding back underachievers, arguing that repeating a grade creates a very stigmatising environment and that students are better off if they are given extra help and if they are tutored by learning specialists.

While very heavy standardised testing is a norm in many countries, the Finnish authorities concluded that such tests cost too much to administer and generate undue stress. The Finnish answer to such testing was to **trust teachers** and to have only a small sample of students sit for exams to keep track of school performance. However, the results of these tests are not made public. Finland has only one set of national exams, when students are about to leave secondary school, aged 18.

Teachers in Finland are given the freedom to design their own courses, and to interpret the subject as they see fit, using a national curriculum as a guide, not a blueprint. If they like, teachers can take their children outside the classroom and learn to add and subtract by counting objects in nature.

Students between the ages of seven and 16 have many classes each week in **sports, arts, music, cooking, carpentry, metalwork and textiles**. The Finnish school day is short and includes ample break time to give children a lot of opportunity to run around and play. Finland has learn the lesson that it is wiser to minimise testing, to invest in more interesting curricula, smaller classes, project work environment, labs and learning based on experiments, and offer better training, pay and treatment of teachers.

EDUCATION OF THE FUTURE

'You may give them your love but not your thoughts, for they have their own thoughts. You may house their bodies but not their souls, for their souls dwell in the house of tomorrow, which you cannot visit, not even in your dreams. You may strive to be like them, but seek not to make them like you. For life goes not backward nor tarries with yesterday.' **Kahlil Gibran, On Children**

We cannot aim to prepare our children for the careers of the future. We live in such a dynamic world that what was a norm 10 years ago, almost certainly will not be reality in 10 years' time.

The education of the future is much more challenging, shifting further away from 'spelling and formulas' towards the development of cognitive thinking where children are given tools to develop their own world, when their time comes.

Apple, Microsoft, Amazon and Google, to name just a few, all started as small companies made up of a few people with an idea, a talent, and motivation to innovate. So, to educate leaders and innovators of the future, we need an education system that nurtures the love of learning and promotes creativity and innovation.

FINLAND IS THIS CENTURY'S ICON OF EDUCATIONAL REFORM SUCCESS

with its students repeatedly gaining the top results in international rankings, Finland is this century's icon of educational reform success. Some four decades after Finland overhauled its educational system, many countries try to learn from its example.

So, what are the lessons we could learn from the Finnish educational model?

FINLAND ONLY HAS PUBLIC SCHOOLS;

The country has closed all the private ones. Before the reform, Finland had large learning differences between schools, with richer students typically outperforming their low-income peers. Today, students do well regardless of their socio-economic status.

THE FINNISH VISION IS THAT EVERY CHILD HAS SOME TALENTS

and those who struggle in certain subjects are given an assistant to help them to progress. No one is left behind. In their educational reform, the Finns first eliminated the practice of separating students into different tracks based on their test scores, and then eliminated examinations altogether. Finnish children never take a standardized test. Tests are not used to compare pupils or teachers or schools to each other.

Children in Finland start primary school at the age of seven.
The idea is that before that time they learn best through play, and by the time they get to the school environment they are keen to start learning.

Teaching is a prestigious career in Finland
and teachers are highly valued. All teachers are required to have higher academic degrees and this guarantees the high quality of teaching. The highly trained teachers have autonomy to make decisions about what and how to teach, they participate in the design of the curriculum of their class, supported by the very lean national standards (featuring fewer than 10 pages of guidance for mathematics, for example).

The Finns also made sure that competent teachers who can shape the best learning conditions for their students are in all the schools.

Teachers keep the same pupils in their classroom for several years.
This helps to develop trust between the teacher and the students.

Children study in a relaxed and informal atmosphere
and teachers use methods that encourage 'thinking', experimenting, project work and collaboration. In a typical classroom, students are not sitting down listening to the teacher; they would be working with other students in small groups, completing projects or writing articles for their own magazine.

The teacher nurtures independence and active learning, allowing students to develop skills to understand and solve problems.

Finnish schools are generally small with relatively small classrooms of around 20 students. All students receive a free meal daily, free health care, transport and learning materials. They also have plenty of holidays – compared to other Europeans, Finnish children spend the fewest number of hours in the classroom.

The success of the Finish model is not within a competition-based environment that is relies heavily on exams, but it is built on the idea that less can be more.

There is a strong emphasis on relaxed schools that nurture creativity, questioning and in-depth subject analysis. Arts, music and sports are an integral part of every child's curriculum. It is interesting that some of the alternative schools founders of the last century, such as Rudolf Steiner and Maria Montessori, have worked on the exact same principles when shaping their schools of the future.

Their knowledge of human nature and child development patterns have influenced the pioneers of educational shift that has been happening in the past few decades. Sir Ken Robinson, an internationally-recognised expert in human creativity, talking about educational reform in the video 'Changing Education Paradigms', invites educational bodies to rethink their policies that advocate competition as the key driver of educational improvement.

FOCUS ON CREATIVITY

Indeed, the Finnish experience shows that a focus on creativity and cooperation can lead to an education system where all children learn well.

ARTS MAKE STUDENTS SMART, CHILDREN AND CREATIVITY

INSPIRING CHILDREN WITH ARTS, MUSIC, SPORT

Arts, sport, music and drama are often viewed as fun extra-curricular activities for children but are given less importance compared with core subjects such as English, science, or mathematics.

Nevertheless, numerous studies prove that practising art, music and sport from an early age improve brain activity, self-confidence, creativity, and gives students an overall sense of well-being.

Students who consistently practice sport, arts, music, drama, and dance, are usually more creative and innovative and also perform better academically.

Physical education programmes can influence the way children view physical fitness when they grow older, how they relate to their body and overall health. Both individual and collective sports require training and strong mental and physical preparation.

Through a wide range of games and activities, children learn teamwork, strategy-building, cooperation and gain much needed confidence.

Many team sports require children to work together to achieve a common goal. They also learn that there is much more to sport than simply winning.

The arts should be taken seriously as a source of inspiration, as a way of life.

ART PROGRAMMES CREATIVITY AND CHILDREN

Art programmes offer much more than just a fun outlet for children; they are an essential element of learning, cultivating self-expression, problem-solving, imagination and creativity.

According to research by **Americans for the Arts** students who undertake three hours of arts, three days a week for at least one year are four times more likely to be recognised for academic achievement.

Furthermore, when **children** are physically active and **creative**, they tend to focus better and work more enthusiastically with the rest of the curriculum.

CHILDREN AND CREATIVITY: EFFECTS OF MUSIC ON THE BRAIN
We all agree that music is a powerful force; it creates deep emotions, and it has been used since man's first beginnings for communication, relaxation and enjoyment.

There is a common misconception that music is only for the chosen few, for talented students to practice and perform.

However, more and more countries include music as an **essential part** of their **countries' curriculum.**

Many studies have been conducted on the **effects of music on the brain**. An exposure to a music programme is likely to benefit a child's ability to concentrate, and it stimulates the development of certain parts of the brain.

EDUCATIONAL CURRICULUM REFORMS MOVING TOWARDS ENHANCING CREATIVITY IN CHILDREN
Various governments have undertaken educational curriculum reforms aimed at expanding **children**'s art, music and sports experience.

An international study of arts education in over 60 countries found that Finland – a leader of education reform worldwide – has far more arts education than any other country. Finnish music schools have more than five times the funding from central government compared to music services in England. The importance of art in Finland is fully recognized and it is woven into their entire education system.

CREATIVITY AS A TANGIBLE ASSET

To move away from the attitudes that do not respect and cultivate arts as core subjects within schools, we should:

• Promote actively the importance of **creativity** as a tangible asset that must be nurtured to benefit the society of the future;

• Actively encourage **music, sport and arts** as subjects that improve creativity and general education of all children;

• Raise the status of music, sport and arts by developing a '**tradition**' within the schools, with the teachers, with the parents, leading to continuous work with performances, concerts, sports events, festivals, and so forth;

• Prepare children for life beyond the school classroom, and have the courage to focus and invest in these areas. **Tests stifle creativity** because questions usually focus on finding one correct answer instead of seeking various ways to solve problems. This inhibits independent thinking and innovation.

A classroom teacher who includes music, sport and arts as an integral part of his teaching methods takes on the role of a conductor, a trainer, an artist, and a researcher, guiding students' exploration towards a deeper understanding of any subject.

Sir Ken Robinson, in his inspirational presentation 'Bring on the learning revolution' on Ted.com, says "we have built our educational system on the model of 'fast food'... where everything is standardized... and this greatly impoverishes our spirit".

ALTERNATIVE SCHOOLING AND CHILDREN CREATIVITY

Waldorf Schools also called Steiner Schools, are based on the educational philosophy of Austrian philosopher Rudolf Steiner.

The methods used are those that stimulate **imagination**, **inspiration**, and **intuition**. Education is practiced **holistically**; handicrafts, the arts, and music are integral parts of the curriculum.

In a holistic educational model the teacher does not 'lecture' but provides space for **children** to **play**, **experiment**, **learn**, and **create**, always keeping a deep connection to life.

For example, children may be asked to write and **illustrate their own textbooks**, a history teacher teaching Renaissance may ask students to make copies of 16th-century scientific instruments, or sing Renaissance operas, or stage a play about 17th-century physicists.

They may study Shakespeare by staging his plays, rotating the cast so that every child memorises a couple of hundred lines.

Even some of the most exclusive private schools in the world today use these 'old fashioned methods' to develop children's capabilities.

They require **every student to learn an instrument**, they teach their students how to play chess, they essentially work on teaching to expand their concentration span.

In such schools, children are encouraged to **question at all stages**, and they seek to **replace competition with collaboration** at every level, developing deep and lasting relationships among their peers and with their teachers.

Schools that inspire children to learn — dream or reality?

For the love of learning

Education is what remains after one has forgotten what one has learnt in school
- Albert Einstein

One can safely assume that all parents have the same goal: that of choosing the best methods for their children to grow into inspired and enthusiastic adults. Helping develop their highest potential, and taking care of each child's development is a dream all parents share.

But unfortunately we are often forced to forget this dream, because of circumstances, lack of knowledge, lack of funds, social pressure to pass exams, or simply because our children are surrounded by teachers who are too tired or not very inspiring.

Albert Einstein's famous quote, " is what remains after one has forgotten what one has learnt in school" leads us to reflect on the possible bottlenecks within the 'traditional' schooling system.

For the love of learning - Alternative schooling

When one talks of alternative schooling, one immediately starts imagining a school that has created a beautiful, inspiring learning space that nurtures harmony and tranquility; one thinks of a school that gives enough importance to sports, music and arts.

One thinks of a school that is open to **different learning methods**, and that goes beyond a national minimum curriculum; one thinks of a school that gives children an opportunity to learn multi-cultural ways of doing things, such as exploring Italian cooking, learning Chinese calligraphy, playing German music, reading Russian classics, creating Japanese ikebana, and so forth.

When one talks of 'alternative schooling', one imagines children returning from school amazed and in awe for what they would have learnt, with a zeal to explore further, with an ability to concentrate and complete their tasks in various circumstances.

One imagines a school that works on the development of the child's 'self' as much as with their understanding of others, that fosters awareness of the inter-**connectedness of all living beings**, that emphasizes the importance of action-based environmental welfare, **taking care of the Earth**, and animals' well-being, including, for example, initiatives such as planting trees, cleaning beaches, walking dogs of sanctuaries.

One imagines that the word '**inspire**' is the middle name of all such schools' activities.

It may sound like a tall order, but in fact there are thousands of schools all around the world that have experimented with alternative educational methods with some very interesting results.

For the love of learning: Waldorf Schools and Creativity

Rudolf , founder of one of these alternative education movements, says "our highest endeavor must be to develop free human beings who are able, of themselves, to impart purpose and direction to their lives".

Schools that have adopted his approach promote the use of only natural materials such as wool, wax, wood and cotton; they encourage their students to create their own books, to cook their lunches together, or bake bread; they learn to dance, they learn mathematics through song, and receive their instruction through fables and poems.

Their vision recognises **each child's freedom and possibility to grow**; these schools emphasise some golden, albeit forgotten methods, such as teaching children to create their own stories, make their own toys, connect with nature by climbing trees or collecting shells, cooking or making own clothes.

These schools believe that these somewhat forgotten 'life-skills' are extremely important for the development of 'complete' personalities.

In contrast with 'fast' education that creates exam-oriented children, many alternative schools are experimenting with a more that uses a mix of tools that develop children's physical, emotional and intellectual capacities.

Some characteristics of alternative schooling
- **Multiple intelligence**
- **Global consciousness**
- **Creative problem solving**
- **High levels of social intelligence**
- **Environmental stewardship**
- **High levels of emotional intelligence**
- **Thinkers who think outside the box**

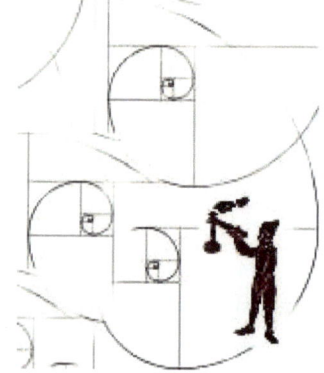

Published by Artof4elements

Artof4Elements is a Publisher based in Malta. Applying Quantum Physics to manifestation of Consciousness researching Ancient History and Philosophy, Artof4Elements has published 44 titles with 8 Authors in English, Italian and French.

About the Author

Nataša Pantović MSc Economics, Maltese Serbian Novelist, Adoptive Parent, and Ancient Worlds' Consciousness Researcher.

Using stories of ancient Greek and Egyptian philosophers and ancient artists, after being Head of Business Development, Consultant and Trainer of 4 largest consulting and IT companies in the UK, Holland, and Malta, I inspire researchers to reach beyond their self-imposed boundaries. Volunteering, I have organized 6 large Body, Mind and Spirit Festivals, I have provided panels for the International Vegetarian Festival, 10 days Conference about Neolithic Temples, and have represented Malta's IT outsourcing, all around the planet. Published author since 1991, with a legal book on Co-operatives, I have helped build a school in a remote village of Ethiopia, and have since adopted two kids, as a single mum: check out our unusual story! In the last five years, with Artof4Elements, have published 2 historical fictions and 7 non-fiction books. Speak English, Serbian, all Balkan Slavic languages, Maltese and Italian.

Born in 1968, in Belgrade, Serbia, worked for many years in Management Consultancy and Executive Management Training. With more than 25 years of experience working with large management consulting companies and consulting independently, major clients include Local Councils, Attorney General of Malta, Education Ministry, Government of Malta, Vodafone Malta, Barclays Kenya, and Safeway UK.

At the moment, I am fascinated by the research into Ancient Europe's Consciousness and Art. Applied Psychology and Philosophy from Tao to Jung, to deeper understand Intuitive Wisdom and Pure Ratio, through the Power of Mind. The AoL publishing include 2 fiction and 5 non-fiction books.

Conscious Parenting: Mindful Living Course for Parents
© Artof4Elements / March 2015

All rights reserved

No part of this book may be reproduced or
transmitted in any form or by any means
without permission in writing from the publisher.
For information address: Artof4Elements

ISBN 978-9995754044

Ivana Milosavljević,
Pantović Nataša,
Conscious Parenting
-English-

Published by Artof4Elements
4, Holly Wood, St. Albert Street, Gzira GZR1157,
Malta

www.artof4elements.com

www.ingramcontent.com/pod-product-compliance
Lightning Source LLC
Chambersburg PA
CBHW040909020526
44116CB00026B/14